Milica Vladova

COMPLETE

BODY

CLEANSING:

Lymph Detox, Juicing Cleanse, Parasite Flush, Kidney Purification, Liver Detox, and more

Milica Vladova
"Complete Body Cleansing: lymph detox, juicing cleanse, parasite flush, kidney purification, liver detox, and more"

Copyright © 2016 by Militsa Vladova

ISBN-13: 978-1548445959

ISBN-10: 1548445959

FREE EBOOKS

Strengthen your immunity, detox, energize, heal, and stimulate your metabolism with these magical potent healthy recipes!

Get your FREE copy of
"10 Powerful Immune Boosting Recipes"
"12 Healthy Dessert Recipes"
"15 Delicious & Healthy Smoothies"
"The Complete Ayurveda Detox"

Go to *www.MindBodyAndSpiritWellbeing.com* and claim your book!

Or simply scan the QR code below:

Dedicated to Rick.

He was more than a dog,

he was a loyal friend and a faithful guardian.

Rest in peace, buddy!

Contents

Introduction

*I*n book 1 we talked about the basics of a natural and gentle detox; how the process works; what the most common modern toxins are and how to decrease our exposure to them. In this book, as a natural sequel, we will dive deep and upgrade our cleansing practices. This book is not intended to be stuffed with fluff just to fill the pages – it is practical, full of recipes, cleansing methods, and tactics you can follow. It will give you tons of ideas you can go back and reference at a later point. It is best to start applying the methods from this book after you have mastered the first steps from the first book. Do not skip or underestimate them! Often we do not really realize how much toxicity we have accumulated over the years. For example, even two cigarettes a day and a glass of wine can burden the liver so much that when we start cleansing this organ, the detox symptoms become unbearable. I am talking about massive headaches, severe nausea and vomiting, dizziness, etc. That is what happened to me a couple of years ago. I was bold and arrogant and thought "Oh, just 3 days on citrus juices? That's a piece of cake!". And soon enough I realized how wrong I was! I couldn't last even a day! The headache was so strong and acute I couldn't even think straight. Then it dawned on me - I had to take a gentler and baby-step approach to get there. My piece of advice to you, so you don't make the same mistakes I did, is to start slow and build on it as you go. You know smart people learn from other's mistakes, and you are smart, I am sure! If you haven't started your healthy living journey, yet, this book may be a bit advanced to you. It is best to start from book 1 and begin applying the principles there first. After you feel comfortable including more fresh fruits and veggies in your diet, getting rid of most toxins, you can go back to this book and continue exploring the more in-depth detox and healing practices.

Do I really need a detox?

*U*hm, yes! Unless, of course, you live in a secluded detached non-polluted area somewhere in the mountains, produce your own bio food, herd goats and drink their fresh milk... Should I go on? No, I am not kidding – the industrialization may be a good thing when it comes to progress, but as far as nature is concerned – we basically screwed up big time! The air we breathe is polluted, the foods we eat are highly processed and full of chemicals, the liquid we drink as well, etc. Even people who tend to live a more balanced and healthy lifestyle need to take regular breaks from food for the digestive system to do its magic – detox and heal. Even the ancient texts advise us to fast regularly to regain our health and energy. Also, there is a wide variety of signs (physical, mental, even emotional) to tell if you definitely need to start cleansing as soon as possible. Or at least begin gently changing your diet habits – it's a good start for the cleansing process. Consider making these diet and lifestyle changes if:

- You have chronic fatigue;
- Your tongue has a thick white coating;
- You have frequent gastrointestinal problems – bloating, acid reflux, flatulence, constipation, etc.
- You have gained a lot of extra weight – especially if it's disproportionate (mainly in the stomach area);
- You have slow metabolism;
- You are frequently irritable and moody;
- You experience severe PMS symptoms;

- You are constantly feeling your liver and gallbladder area tight and heavy or you have some other similar sensations;
- You have strange and unpleasant body smell or bad breath;
- You suffer from insomnia;
- You have brain fog, difficulty concentrating;
- You constantly get skin rashes, acne, itches and unnatural darker complexion (grayish);
- You have cellulite;
- You experience constant mucus secretion – from the nose, lungs, vulva;
- You have puffy eyes or dark circles;
- Your immunity is weak and unstable – frequent colds, flu, allergies, etc.

But before jumping into conclusions, it is best to consult with a physician and to run some tests if needed. These symptoms could mean something else. Just don't become a hypochondriac! In most cases the real culprit is our own unhealthy lifestyle and choices, and that's totally manageable! So, do not worry, with persistence and consistency everything is achievable!

So, what could be achieved?

Having a cleaner and healthier diet and lifestyle can become a profound life changer! And not just in the health and fitness area! Just think about it – if you don't have enough energy and focus, how are you supposed to run a successful business? Maintain healthy relationships? Travel and have fun? Play with your kids? Enjoy life?

Starting the detoxification process can be difficult and uncomfortable, but once you go through the detox crisis, you will really feel the difference, the lightness, the vitality, the mental clarity... And you don't even have to experience these detox discomforts. If you incorporate the habits in book 1, chances are your body is prepared for the deeper cleansing methods described in this volume.

By consistently practicing even the tiniest cleansing tricks, you can significantly boost your energy, clear your skin, improve your immunity, get more focused and clear-minded, improve your sleep, get calmer and happier, slow down aging (yay!), even surprisingly – develop your intuition!

Speaking of intuition, here is a special note for people interested in spirituality: cleansing the body is a very important step in enhancing our energetic level and broadening our consciousness. Regular detox clears our spiritual "antennas" and we become more capable of reconnecting with our source (God, the Universe, or whatever you may want to call it). Most famous spiritual gurus in the past and the present were/are fasting regularly and leading a vegetarian life. Saint Francis of Assisi is one of these examples – he had been reported to levitate above the ground after his regular religious and spiritual fasting period. In the section below you will learn some exciting results (physical and spiritual) people get when detoxing regularly.

How do I start?

As I said, (and I will continue to nag about it because it is important) it is best to start slowly from little baby steps until you get a handle of the process and prepare your body for a detox revolution! Here is what I would suggest. (My Virgo ascendant is taking charge and we are starting to get practical right from the start! I told you there would be no fluff! :D)

1. *Start by eliminating your toxin intake* – identify which of the most common toxins is your weakest spot. Do you have a sweet tooth? Or maybe you really like eating white flour pastries? Do you overindulge in coffee, energy drinks or alcohol? Start from there and build on it until you feel comfortable with your new toxin-free behavior.

2. *Take it easy* – do not rush in the eliminating process. Your body needs time to accommodate and get used to the new behavior. Otherwise, you will feel constant cravings for unhealthy foods and drinks. So, don't get over ambitious and listen to your body.

3. *Include some daily detox habits*, like lemon water, or green smoothies, etc. Whatever feels good and easy to start with.

4. Next, *try some weekly detox rituals.* In this volume you will get tons of ideas.

5. *Continue with the colon* – if you have been suffering from chronic constipation, and you haven't found the solution from your daily cleansing habits, it is best to pay extra attention to this area. We need to boost the digestive system and clear the passage for toxins to be

flushed out easily. We have to ensure there are no road blocks in their way out.

6. After you clean the colon, you can **focus on the liver**, because it is an essential part of the detox process. We cannot help the body cleanse itself with a clogged liver (and gallbladder).

7. **Continue with one of your problem areas** and experiment with different approaches according to your needs and preferences. For example, if you constantly have a clogged nose from excess mucus, go to the chapter dedicated to this problem.

8. **Prepare your mind** – before starting a detox, you need to be mentally prepared – affirm to yourself you can do this and visualize the positive outcome. The biggest problem with sticking to our new diets and healthy lifestyles is not physical, it's mental. Our minds need to be prepared and calm in the process for it to work long term.

9. **Clear up your schedule** – it is best to perform these detox rituals in a calm home environment during your days off, especially if you try some new unfamiliar approach. You never know how your body may react. I remember the first time I tried a rice&apple weekly detox, and the next day I didn't expect to have such overactive colon at all! Needless to say, I couldn't go out for a walk outside that day. (chuckle)

10. **Prepare your products** – plan your detox routine the day before, so you don't stress about it on the actual date.

11. **Don't try to do everything** – this book is packed with detox rituals and recipes, but don't get overwhelmed! Start small and dip your toes in the

water to see what appeals to you. We are all different and our needs and tolerance levels vary.

12. ***Listen to your body*** – your body is your greatest ally, treat it with respect and always listen to its signals. It may take some time to distinguish if it is really your body speaking or the sugar craving, or the detox symptoms. Judge your feelings after you have tested a method for some time.

13. In case you have any chronic illnesses, or you take any prescription medications, it is best to ***consult with your physician*** before embarking on a deep detox. In most cases, the cleansing will help the body heal and restore its natural healthy state, but the detox method needs to be suitable for your condition. It is always a good idea to talk to a naturopathic doctor who can guide you in the right direction.

14. ***No pregnant/breastfeeding women please!*** The detox methods in this volume are not suitable for you. The toxins you will eliminate will get into the bloodstream, the milk, and into the baby's system. Wait until your precious offspring is weaned off the breastfeeding.

Well, enough chit-chatting! Let's get down to business.

WEEKILY DETOX

RITUALS

Weekly detox rituals

After we have mastered the gentle toxin elimination process and incorporated long-lasting healthy habits in our lifestyle, we can continue including more gentle methods and strategies in our detoxing arsenal. These techniques it is best to be applied on a weekly basis for a long period of time. They usually last a day or two, so they won't be a huge challenge. But do not underestimate them – if executed regularly, they can make a tremendous difference in your health, energy levels, and appearance. You will be wondering where the extra pounds went. And remember, detox is not all about losing weight and shredding fat. The fat is just the body's protection tool to disarm harmful toxins from damaging our system. When we slowly incorporate such gentle methods of detoxing little by little, our bodies no longer need the fat to protect us. And the best part is – the process happens effortlessly without any harsh detox symptoms or discomforts. That is why I love weakly detox!

These methods can be applied at any time of the year as a sustaining and enhancing tool for your healthy lifestyle!

Let's begin!

Weekly fasting day with water/tea

Sometimes we do not have control over the food we intake. Or our lifestyle cannot support the changes we want to install. Or maybe we just want to accelerate the cleansing process. This is why one fasting day a week can have a such positive impact. The principle is easy – one day a week we abstain from eating anything solid and we drink lots of water or detox tea. In this way the immune system located in the intestines will be engaged only in detoxing the body, instead of absorbing and breaking down nutrients. In the meantime, the water and tea will take most of the toxins out of the body. The downside to this method is that it is not suitable for everybody. Some people (especially those with low blood pressure or low blood sugar) may experience unpleasant sensations. For everybody else, take a look at all the benefits of regular fasting:

- **Boosts our immunity** (a large part of our immune system is located in the guts);
- **Lowers the blood sugar level** – sadly, the modern diet consists of large quantities of white sugar and white flour products, which constantly raise our blood sugar level. *Note: people with very low blood sugar levels and insulin dependent diabetics should perform fasting only under medical surveillance!*
- **Has an anti-aging effect** – the healthier our body is, the longer we will keep our young appearance;
- **Protects the brain** – here is what Dr. Mark Mattson (Chief of the Laboratory of Neuroscience at the National Institute on Aging) found about the effect of intermittent fasting on our brain:
  "Challenges to your brain, whether it's intermittent fasting [or] vigorous exercise . . . is cognitive challenges. When this happens, neuro-circuits are activated, levels of neurotrophic factors increase, that promotes the growth of neurons [and] the formation and strengthening of synapses... Intermittent fasting enhances the ability of nerve cells to repair DNA. "
  If scientists confirm it, who am I to argue?

- **Protects the heart** – fasting regularly for short periods of time can significantly lower the cholesterol plaques accumulation and improve the whole cardiovascular system.

Ekadashi – the best day for a fasting detox

We all know how the Moon governs the movement of water and fluids on Earth and in our bodies as well. And since we consist of more than 70% water, the Moon cycle is essential for keeping our health and wellbeing. No wonder our ancestors paid close attention to this celestial body, planned their agriculture according to its movement, and even worshiped it. They knew how important it is for us and all the natural processes on Earth.

The 4 Moon phases are: from New Moon to First Quarter, from First Quarter to Full Moon, from Full Moon to Third Quarter, and from Third Quarter to New Moon. Each of these phases has a different effect on our physiology through the movement of body fluids and hormone secretion. For example, during phase 1 and 3 our bodies are in absorption mode. This period is excellent for nourishing the tissues and the skin with natural oil massages, mineral and essential oil bubble baths, etc. During phases 2 and 4 the opposite processes are activated – the body takes out more easily than it absorbs. These are the magical moments to do fasting detoxes, and enemas to flush out all unnecessary components out of our system.

The most potent days from these phases are the Ekadashi days (the 11th and the 26th Lunar day) and the Two pipes (14th Lunar day)[1]. According to Ayurveda these are the

---

[1] You can find the exact date and time for the Ekadashi in every Moon

best days to perform your regular fasting detox. It will have the best effect not only for the body, but for our spirituality as well. The ancient Indian texts state that during Ekadashi it is best to abstain from any solid food for 24-36 hours. If taking only water is too harsh for you, you can add some tea or fruit/vegetable juice (without the pulp!). The energy we save from digestion will be directed to healing our tissues and enhancing our spirituality. This is the perfect opportunity to meditate, pray, read, or just experience Oneness.

The Two Pipes day is a little bit different. Here Ayurveda advises us to perform the fasting without any liquids. If this is difficult or impossible for you, just keep the liquid in the smallest possible dosages. Also there is another interesting mystical detail about this day – it is said that all new endeavors should be started on this day. That is how you can ensure they will be successful. What an excellent day to start your new healthier and more vital lifestyle!

Weekly fasting day with green smoothies

If one day with no food is too extreme for you or it does not suit your physical status, you can try an easier version – one day only on green smoothies. Green smoothies made such a huge health revolution! And no wonder! They are powerful energy bombs – full of vitamins, microelements, fiber, etc. The fruits and vegetables inside are very easy to digest, so the immune system can still work on cleansing our bodies. Moreover, they supply more water which helps the process even more. And you don't have to worry about the

calendar or the special Ekadashi Lunar calendars you can find on the web.

carbohydrates too much – the fiber from the pulp slows down the absorption of glucose, so there are no big insulin rushes. You can find so many different recipes or make your own favorite blends. The only things you need are a blender and fruits and leafy greens of your choice. Don't worry if your blender is not top notch – it is even better that way. The green smoothies must be "chewed" instead of drunk in large gulps. So, if your blender cannot make the liquid perfectly smooth, you will be forced to chew it and therefore – digest it even more easily. You can even add whatever super foods you like – bee pollen, chia, flax powder, goji berry, etc. *One precaution when drinking smoothies: rinse your mouth with plain or salty water afterwards.* The fructose in the fruits (especially citrus ones) can damage the tooth enamel and cause teeth sensitivity. This piece of advice applies for every type of carbs we eat – honey, sugar, bread, even apple cider vinegar. *Don't brush your teeth, though, only rinse your mouth. Brushing the teeth after eating something acidic is like brushing your hair when it's wet – it is fragile and can be easily damaged.*

Here is one simple detoxing recipe you might like:

Yummy pear&coconut detox drink

Ingredients:
- o *1 1/2 cup* **almond milk**
- o *2* **pears**
- o *fistful of* **fresh St.John's wort**
- o *1 Tbsp.* **coconut butter**
- o *1 Tbsp.* **flax seed powder**
- o *2 Tbsps.* **Hemp seeds**
- o *a pinch of* **Cayenne pepper** *(optional)*

Directions:
Simply place all ingredients in a blender and puree them until you have a homogenous mixture. Enjoy!

Rice & Fruits day
If you feel uncomfortable to start a detox procedure abstaining from food, you can try this simple method. All you need is 50-100 g (half cup) rice, preferably brown rice, 1-2 kilos apples (or any other fruits you like) and 2 liters pure warm water or unsweetened tea. Simply boil the rice in 1 liter water; you may add some parsley, fennel, diet salt, lemon juice, or other vegetables, but do not add any fat. Divide the rice and the fruits into 5 portions for each meal. And that's it! These apple-rice days are perfect for people with high blood pressure, and women suffering from PMS. The rice absorbs the Sodium from the body, which is the main cause of water retaining. In this way we take all unnecessary water and toxins out of our system.

Why brown rice?

If you have to choose between white and brown rice, I would advise you to pick the brown one. These two kinds of foods have some differences and it's not just their color. The main important contrast is that brown rice is whole grain unlike the white one. White rice is a processed food, stripped from its shell and therefore has lost some of its natural beneficial nutrients. In this line of thought, brown rice is closer to its natural state. Keeping the grain's coat, we also keep its fiber, vitamins, and minerals. Speaking of fiber, I hear a lot of people underestimating its significance. *"We don't need cellulose, because we cannot digest it!"* Actually, that's just half true. Yes, we cannot break down the insoluble fiber unlike ruminants. But we need cellulose for physically cleansing the colon – it acts like a brush to the colon's walls, preventing us from constipation and cancer cells formation. Fiber also slows down the digestion of carbohydrates and thus keeping the blood sugar and insulin at low levels. (Brown rice has a much lower glycemic index than the white grain). And we know how important that is for our health and slender silhouette.

Here are just a few of the many health benefits of brown rice. If you include this unrefined grain in your menu (or even better – do the rice & fruits detox regularly), you will significantly lower the risk of developing hypertension, diabetes and its consequences. Brown rice is rich in Selenium, which reduces the risk of developing cancer, arthritis, cardiovascular, and thyroid diseases.

Moreover, it has a lot of Manganese, which plays an important part in the breaking down of fats in our bodies. It also boosts the work of the reproductive systems for both men and women.

Eat brown rice often and it will help you combat age, free radicals, and disease-causing microorganisms for its good amount of antioxidants.

Drink your rice water!

As I mentioned earlier, when preparing your rice for this cleansing method keep the bullion and drink it throughout the day. As you may have guessed, when we boil plants, herbs, grains, etc., some of their nutrients, vitamins, and minerals will go into the water. So, our rice decoction will have some beneficial health values. Here are some of them: rice water contains essential amino acids, Vitamins B1, B2 and B3 (niacin), as well as Potassium, Zinc, Iron and Selenium. These compounds help our bodies cope with stress, prevent cancer, and keep the thyroid gland in good shape. Rice water is especially useful for children because it is easily digestible. It also promotes probiotics and beneficial colon bacteria to multiply, boosting our immune system.

In short, rice water:
- *is the number one natural remedy for nausea and vomiting;*
- *helps tremendously against gastroenteritis and diarrhea;*
- *regulates the blood pressure;*
- *helps the prevention of Alzheimer's disease and cancer;*
- *stimulates the blood circulation;*

- tones the body (because of the high content of complex carbohydrates);
- reduces the body temperature;
- is excellent for people suffering from anemia;
- fights the flu, etc.

Variation with vegetable juice

In this section I will share with you a small variation of this rice detox which I use regularly with great success. I include 3 more things beside the fruits and the brown rice – detox tea, vegetable juice and a salad. I will describe the method step by step so you can follow through or adjust it to your schedule and needs.

First off I start the day with a detox tea on an empty stomach. Peppermint, Thyme, Green tea, Rooibos are excellent options.

So, let's say you get up at 07:00 AM and drink your tea at 07:30. Hot tea in the morning usually has a nice gentle laxative effect.

In one or two hours prepare the vegetable juice. I use one bulb beetroot, several carrots and a small piece of ginger. This combination had gained my love and respect because of its powerful energizing and detoxing effect. Plus, it is a natural laxative and the next day it will be extremely easy for you to empty and cleanse the intestines. But feel free to experiment and try different combinations according your taste. All edible rhizomes are wonderful immune stimulators and detoxifiers.

The beetroot juice nicely satisfies the appetite, so in two hours you can have the first portion of the fruits. It is OK to feel slightly hungry; we need to give the digestive system a break to do its detoxing job properly. You can have whatever fruits you choose, preferably seasonal bio organic ones. I also advise you to always include apples in the mix. Apples are one of the best choices for cleansing the body and especially the guts. Later in this book you will find the wonderful detoxing effect of apple pectin.

After you have taken the fruit portion, wait for another 2 hours (or more) and take your first brown rice meal. Remember to eat slowly and to chew properly.

Continue interchanging between fruit and rice meals every two hours or so. Remember not to overeat, and drink plenty of water or unsweetened herbal tea between the meals.

At the end of the day, you can have a nice fiber rich salad. Choose the vegetables you like or the ones that are currently available. Leafy greens, cabbage, rhizomes are wonderful choices. Season the salad with some apple cider vinegar, extra virgin olive oil (or other cold pressed oil), and some diet salt (sea or Himalayan salt). The fiber in the salad will further sweep away food debris and fecal stones from the intestines like a brush.

Weekly Detox & Healing Recipe

This recipe is developed to gently cleanse the body, stimulate the natural immunity, and to promote long and healthy life. It is very easy to make and the ingredients are not so exotic.

Ingredients:
- o   2 Tbsps. **lemon juice;**
- o   5 grams **fresh grated ginger;**
- o   2 Tbsps. **honey;**
- o   A pinch of **cayenne pepper;**
- o   A pinch of **anise;**
- o   2 liters **pure water.**

Directions:

Bring the water to boil, and let it simmer for 5 minutes. After that, let it cool off to room temperature. Place all ingredients in the water and stir well. Wait for at least 30 minutes and you can drink from this infusion. Take one cup of the liquid before each meal or as much as you like throughout the day.

Epsom salt baths

Bathing in water is beneficial for our bodies, especially when it comes to detoxing. It can also have a profound effect on our spirituality by cleansing our aura from stuck negative energy. Adding Epsom salt (Magnesium Sulfate) to our regular bubble baths will enhance this effect even more. Magnesium is an excellent detoxing mineral. It also strengthens our nervous system and boosts our immunity.

Why in the bath tub?

This mineral is more easily absorbed through the skin rather than orally. That is why when we apply it on our derma; we make the process more effective and quick. Clearing our physical and energetic toxins with Epsom salts will boost the magnetic field of the body thus boosting the aura. If you don't have a bath tub, you can use a homemade

Epsom salt exfoliator. Just mix some Magnesium salts with a little carrier oil of choice! Just rub it gently on clear skin, wait for it to be absorbed and wash off with some warm water.

Variation 1 with ginger

Ginger is a wonderful plant which has been used in natural medicine for many years now. It is one of the strongest detoxifiers and an absolute must for purifying the body. The root contains a substance called gingerol – a compound which has acute anti-inflammatory and anti-spasmodic properties. Combining the ginger abilities and the reverse osmosis method from the Epsom salt solution, we get the perfect detoxing (and relaxing) bath. Here is what you will need:

Ingredients;
- o   1/2 cup **ginger powder;**
- o   1 Tbsp. **Epson salt;**
- o   1 Tbsp. **ground ginger root;**
- o   A few drops **ginger essential oil**

Directions:

Add all ingredients in the hot water and stir well. Soak in the bath tub for 20-30 minutes and wash the body with plain water and mild non-toxic soap.

You can repeat the procedure every week.

You may notice heavy sweating even after the bath, this is normal – the detoxing process had been activated.

Don't forget to drink plenty of water to facilitate the cleansing.

Variation 2 with Bentonite clay

The detoxing properties of Bentonite clay are undeniable. You will find more about this magical clay later in this book. For now I will share with you how to gently cleanse the body with this muddy bath on a weekly basis.

Ingredients:
- o 1/2 cup **Bentonite clay**
- o 1/2 cup **warm water**
- o 1 cup **Epsom salt**
- o A few drops of **your favorite essential oil(s)**

Directions:
Mix the clay and the warm water well. *Remember: do not use any metal utensils or containers when dealing with Bentonite clay!*

Dissolve the Epsom salt in some water, too.

Put the homogenous mud and the Magnesium solution (the Epsom salt water) in the hot tub and stir well. Add the chosen essential oil, and the bath is ready.

Soak for 20 minutes or so and wash your skin.

Essential oils for detox

Using essential oils for our cleansing routines is an extremely pleasant and refreshing way to expel toxins from our bodies. All natural pure organic oils have some benefits for us, but some of these herbal extracts are better equipped for assisting our detox process. Here I will list the best ones for this purpose:

a. ***Peppermint essential oil*** – this common oil can be applied on the skin or it can be drunk diluted in some water. **Only pure organic essential oils are suitable for consumption!** Use only the ones from a trusted source. If this option seems too extreme for you, do not hesitate to use this essential oil in various natural skin products or massages. Peppermint has refreshing, warming/cooling and stimulating effects. It can relieve symptoms such as sinusitis, mental fatigue, nausea, toothache, stomach pain, neuralgia, migraine, headache, varicose veins, motion sickness, and it can be applied for improving concentration as well;

b. ***Rosemary essential oil*** – this natural oil is perfect for cleansing the body – it helps the work of our overall systems and organs. Stimulates the blood flow and digestion, it has distinct anti-inflammatory and diuretic properties. It also has stimulating, strengthening and warming effects. Rosemary essential oil is applied for treating anemia, muscle atrophy, low blood pressure, colitis, lethargy, hysteria, hangover, migraine, arthritis, stiffness, neuralgia, respiratory problems, seborrhea, and even weak memory. Some naturopaths even state that Rosemary oil fights and prevents from cancer cell development.

c. ***Tangerine essential oil*** – this oil is made from the fruit's skin, which holds great detoxing properties. It gently stimulates and cleanses the liver, which is one of the most important organs regarding body detox. The oil has sedative and pain relieving properties. It can successfully be applied as an appetite and digestion stimulator (in cases of anorexia), for hormonal imbalances, constipation, insomnia, anxiety, depression, hysteria, and tension. When applied on the skin in various lotions or during a massage, it can heal contaminated skin, stretch marks, and even scars.

d. *Lemon essential oil* – this is a great essential oil for boosting our immune system, stimulating the lymph flow, fighting inflammations, and even dealing with cancer. It also has purifying, firming and toning effects. Lemon oil stimulates the blood circulation, ejects the toxins and uric acid out of the body. It can successfully be used for conditions such as arthritis, rheumatism, bronchitis, catarrh, asthma, warts, and headaches.

e. *Patchouli essential oil* – one little known herb, which gains more and more popularity, and it definitely deserves it! This essential oil stimulates the reproductive organs and hormones. It gently cleanses the body with its slight diuretic effect, even if it is applied directly on the skin. The oil also has purifying, meditative and relaxing properties. It is used for firming the skin, as an aphrodisiac, against frigidity, muscle cramps, respiratory problems, acne, athlete's foot, wrinkles, enlarged pores, and weeping eczemas.

f. *Juniper essential oil* – this oil is extracted from the fruits of the Juniper tree. It contains lots of antioxidants, which slow down the aging process, fight the free radicals, and cleanse the body. It soothes the nervous system, alleviates anxiety, nervous tension, and mental exhaustion. It is an excellent assistant in dealing with an enlarged prostate, and helps people with kidney stones or cystitis to urinate more easily. Juniper essential oil is one of the best oils to treat cellulitis, and water retention. It also gently stimulates the digestive system, fights obesity and bloating from PMS. It tones the liver (promoting detox), and regulates the menstrual cycle. Reduces the uric acid in the joints, which makes it perfect for people with gout, arthritis, and rheumatism. Apply this essential oil on the skin to treat acne, eczemas, and even psoriasis.

Do not forget to avoid using citrus essential oils before exposing to the sun! This can cause hyper pigmentation. You can find more information about the use and precautions about essential oils in my first book *"Toxin-free Homemade Easy Beauty Recipes"*.

Here is an interesting recipe with essential and carrier oils you can easily prepare at home. As you progress with this book, you will find out why applying pure natural oils helps us detox even from the most stubborn toxins. Or you can jump right into the section dedicated to the Complete Ayurvedic detox and the self-massage cleansing routine.

For starters you can follow this simplified method. Take 20 ml natural cold pressed oil (jojoba, hazelnut, olive oil, peach oil, etc.) and add several drops essential oil (bergamot, orange, clove, oregano, cedar, lavender, lemon, silver-fir, chamomile, pine, thyme, eucalyptus, and so on). Massage the skin gently with circular movements until the skin absorbs most of the oil. Some of the "heavier" oils may not be fully absorbed, so you need to wash it off with warm water.

Kitchari

Kitchari is a traditional Ayurvedic recipe for a gentle detox. According to the ancient Indian natural medicine, the most important part of healing is prevention. And the best prevention happens when we take out all toxic substances from the body and balance the three main human constitutions (doshas) – Vata, Pitta, and Kapha. You don't need to know your type to use Kitchari at your advantage. It is suitable for each one of them, because it gently balances them all. Kitchari is a good example of gentle body cleanse where you don't need to starve and experience harsh detox symptoms. It is extremely suitable for people with problematic digestion. The main ingredients in this recipe are rice, mung beans, ghee, and some spices. Even people with slow metabolism can take this dish for it is easily digestible. It uses only white rice or the Basmati type, because brown rice may cause some irritation for people with sensitive stomachs. The other main ingredient is the Mung beans. You can use the green or yellow ones. Use the green type if you have strong digestion, and soak it overnight. The yellow one has its skin removed, so it is more suitable for people with poor digestion and sensitive stomachs. Beside their excellent nutritional value, the best thing about these beans is, unlike the other types of legumes, they do not cause bloating and flatulence. Moreover, its taste is far sweeter than the most common beans.

When it comes to nutrition, Kitchari is perfectly balanced – it contains a combination of carbohydrates and amino acids. The rice supplies the important carbohydrates and amino acids such as methionine, tryptophan, and cysteine. On the other hand, the beans contribute with the essential protein lysine. The third main ingredient is also very important – pure ghee butter. According to Ayurveda this pure fatty substance extracts the toxins accumulated in the body, and takes them out through the gastrointestinal tract. The spices, which had been dissolved in the butter, will enhance this process with their natural healing and cleansing properties. So, just to recap – this detoxing meal is an excellent alternative for those who are not able to do harsh cleansing procedures, which usually involve abstaining from food. Let's begin!

Traditional Indian Detoxing Recipe (Kitchari)

Ingredients:

- o *2-4 Tbsp.* **Ghee** *(do not worry, I will describe how to prepare it)*
- o *1/4 cup* **yellow or soaked green Mung beans**
- o *1/2 cup* **white or Basmati rice**
- o *1/2 tsp* **cumin**
- o *1/2 tsp* **asafetida powder**
- o *1/2 tsp* **turmeric powder**
- o *1/2 tsp* **dried ginger powder**
- o *1 tsp* **coriander**
- o *3 bay leaves*
- o *1/2 tsp* **salt**
- o *4 cups* **hot pure water**
- o *some* **fresh green herbs** *(parsley, mint, dill) - optional*

Preparation:

Put the ghee butter in a metal pot and heat it with medium heat temperature. Add all spices (except the salt) and stir for a couple of seconds. Add the rice and Mung beans and stir thoroughly, so that all ingredients mix well. Quickly after that add the hot water and bring it boil. After the mixture begins to simmer, put the lid on the pot and lower the heat. Do not open the lid and do not stir the dish for the next 5-7 minutes. The steam is essential for the preparation of Kitchari. Next, we open the pot, add the salt, and test the beans if they are well boiled. If not, add some more water, put the lid back on, and wait for several more minutes for them to be fully cooked. When the dish is ready, take it off the heat and season it with some fresh spices (if you have at the moment) – dill, parsley, mint, coriander, etc.

Benefits:

What benefits can we reap from this simple, but powerful Ayurvedic meal? Well, first of all, it is a gentle cleansing recipe, which won't cause big detox symptoms (headaches, dizziness, nausea, irritability, even heart palpitations). One of the main reasons for this is the low blood sugar level during harsh fasting and detoxing programs. Kitchari can help us avoid these painful experiences and cleanse our bodies at the same time. **However, should you have any serious illnesses, do not hesitate to consult with your physician, or nutritionist to discuss with them which gentle cleansing procedures are good for you.**

If you like this recipe, you can start adding this meal in your weekly gentle cleansing plan. For example, one day of the week you can take only Kitchari with some ginger tea. For best results combine the inner "oiling" (ghee) with the external one – applying detoxing massages (see the previous section on essential oils). This combination is called Purva-karma and it is the preparation of the complete Ayurvedic detox process. We will discuss this in the annual detoxing rituals section.

How to make your own ghee?

You can find ghee butter already prepared in the health stores. Choose the brands you trust, that use only pure ingredients. It is advisable that the milk, from which the butter is prepared, comes from free range animals fed with clean food, and not treated with chemicals and medications. If you have local farmers who produce such kind of clean milk products, it best to use it instead the store-bought. Here I will describe how to turn the regular butter into the purified ghee. Note the recipe, because you may need it for the other types of Ayurvedic cleansing methods we are going to explore later. Ghee is one of the best fatty products you can have in your home. Let's begin!

Take 1 kilo pure high quality unsalted butter. Cut it into smaller cubes so that it will melt faster. Next, we put the butter cubes in a metal pot with thick bottom. Melt the butter on low temperature, so that it won't burn. When it becomes liquid, increase the temperature in order for it to start boiling. When the butter starts to form bubbles, lower the temperature and let it simmer for a while. Next you will see foam forming on top of the liquid. Remove it gently and carefully with a slotted spoon. You will notice how the butter becomes clearer and clearer, its color turns into nice amber, and its smells really appealing (if the butter is pure and high quality). When the liquid is all cleared up (it may take even an hour), take it off the heat, and let it cool off. Next, strain it through cheesecloth, and put it in a glass container with a tight lid (jar). Let the butter cool off completely, and then you can seal it with the lid, otherwise the water in it will condense. Do not store in a refrigerator, and be extremely careful not to let any water get in the jar. Always scoop from the butter with a clean dry utensil! From 1 kilo butter, you may get about 800 grams pure ghee. If you follow all preparation and storing instructions diligently, the ghee butter must not spoil. It may last even for 100 years, as

Ayurveda specialists say. Actually, old homemade ghee is an extremely precious and expensive product in India. Some families pass it from generation to generation and use it in their special Vedic rituals, or for disease prevention, and healing. Now it is a good time to discover some of its wonderful beneficial properties!

Why ghee is so important?

If you dive deep into the Indian culture, cuisine, and traditional natural medicine, you will notice how ghee plays an integral part in all of them. Let's explore some of its amazing holistic benefits! This purified butter is very easy to digest, even for people with lactose intolerance, because during the purification process we eliminate the milk protein called casein. Ghee is suitable for all dosha types – it gently balances them, slows down the aging process, and promotes the natural body cleansing processes. It stimulates the digestion, and helps people with all kinds of problems in this area. The Ayurveda specialists call these cases – weak digestive fire. Moreover, this gentle dairy product soothes the nervous system, stimulates the memory, boosts the metabolism and our immunity, and enhances our energetic field (the aura).

One of the best parts of ghee is that it is universal – you can use it internally or externally. I will give you some examples here.

- o For **prevention and building immunity** you can take it in the morning on an empty stomach;

o For **healing digestive problems** you can mix it with some herbs and spices like fennel, pepper, cinnamon, cardamom, etc.

o For **soothing anxiety and insomnia** you can massage the body or the feet before going to bed.

Detoxing with Diatomaceous earth

What is Diatomaceous earth (or simply Diatomite)?

It is a *"naturally occurring, soft, siliceous sedimentary rock that is easily crumbled into a fine white to off-white powder... Diatomaceous earth consists of fossilized remains of diatoms, a type of hard-shelled algae."*[2] Diatomaceous earth is highly absorbent and it is a perfect and harmless detoxing agent. When it enters the stomach, it reacts with the stomach acids forming a biologically active orthosilicic acid, which is easily digestible. Diatomaceous earth (just like Bentonite clay) is negatively charged – it magnetically attracts the positively charged bacteria, viruses, toxins, pesticides, food and chemical debris, heavy metals, and takes them out without burdening our bodies. It gently cleanses the gastrointestinal tract without harming the mucosa or the beneficial colon bacteria.

Benefits of Diatomite

This natural Silicon source has a plethora of beneficial effects on the human body. Along with detoxing our cells, it stimulates the metabolism and promotes the healthy weight

[2] Source: Wikipedia

loss. If you have any of these physical discomforts, Diatomite may be your best assistant:

- o *Arthritic pain in the back and joints;*
- o *Low immunity and chronic fatigue;*
- o *Skin issues like eczemas, psoriasis, rashes;*
- o *Slow healing wounds and bones;*
- o *Predisposition to respiratory diseases;*
- o *Allergies;*
- o *Hypertension;*
- o *Constipation;*
- o *Intestinal parasites;*
- o *Insomnia, etc.*

And all these benefits from one single essential microelement – Silicon. In the past humans had plenty of this element due to the natural agriculture, but now things are different. Nowadays most of us have a Silicon deficiency and our bodies react with the above mentioned negative experiences.

Here is how to replenish our Silicon and detox with Diatomite:

The good thing about this substance is that it breaks down easily in water and it is not accumulated in the body when ingested. So, you can simply dilute it in some water, juice, yogurt, smoothies, coconut water, etc.

The dosage for adults starts with 1 tsp. a day (in the morning on an empty stomach 30 minutes before breakfast or **before taking any medications, supplements or vitamins**). For small children, it starts with 1/4 tsp.

Diatomite. Stir well before each sip, because it quickly deposits at the bottom of the glass. Slowly increase the dosage to 1 Tbsp. for adults and 1 tsp. for kids. Listen to your body.

Important note: always take food grade Diatomaceous earth – this is the purest and safest type for consumption.

MONTHLY DETOX

RITUALS

Monthly Detox Rituals

*I*f you want to take the purification process even a step further, you can take a couple of days a month to cleanse the body more effectively. You certainly don't need to do it every single month. Listen to your body and it will tell you when you need to take that step. The best time to do your monthly detox is in spring (March-April) when the body is waking up from the winter, and in the autumn (October-November) when the body is preparing for the upcoming harsh cold months. Of course, detoxification is welcome at any given time in the year, especially if you have some of the symptoms of high toxicity levels, or if you want to feel lighter and calmer. Here is what you can apply to achieve that:

Three Day Citrus Juice Cleanse

Short-term abstinence from food is an important part of keeping our bodies healthy. Even the purest foods engage the immune system, and it needs periods of rest in order for it to work perfectly. And eighty percent of our immune system is located in our intestines.

This cleansing procedure continues for 3 consecutive days for it to give the body the necessary time to detox and flush out all unneeded chemicals. To enhance this method, try to do the cleansing process during the full Moon phase. During this period the body flushes out the toxins much easily along with the taken fluids (fruit juice) and the fasting becomes much easier. If we abstain from solid food for a short period of time, our organism can cleanse up to 12 liters of body fluids full of toxins, helping the work of the lymphatic system. There is also a beneficial external effect – losing weight (depending on the level of toxicity of the body, you can lose even up to 7 extra kilos for 3 days).

The first thing in the morning is to take 10-15 g Epsom salt dissolved in 50-70 ml pure water. Epsom salt is not absorbed by our bodies; it draws out the fluids into the colon by the process of reverse osmosis. Half an hour later, we start with the fruit juice. It is made from freshly squeezed citrus fruits – 2-3 lemons, 4-6 grapefruits, and as many oranges needed to reach a total of 2 liters of fruit liquid. Mix the juice with 2 liters of pure water and the cleansing juice is ready. Keep in mind that citrus fruits can damage the tooth enamel. To avoid ruining your teeth, swish your mouth with clean or salty water after consuming fruits or other sugary foods (including vinegar and wine). If you don't want to use citruses for this cleansing procedure, you can swap them with fresh apple juice. No solid food should be taken during these 3 days. If you feel severe starving, you can have some fruits.

Repeat this for two more days, and it is best the last day of the detox to be during the Full Moon. On the fourth day, you can start adding solid food to your diet. Do not rush this part of the cleansing – it is essential. Have a light breakfast with fresh fruits and vegetables. Later, you can have a second breakfast with some oatmeal. For example, you can mix 2-3 Tbsp. of oatmeal with 1 Tbsp. oat bran and soak them in warm water (avoid using milk at this stage). For lunch, have some boiled potatoes with a salad (without vinegar). For dinner, it is best to have some steamed vegetables.

One word of caution, during any type of deep body cleansing, there may be different uncomfortable side effects –

headaches, nausea, fatigue, etc. These symptoms are normal and only temporal. After the detox, you can notice the benefits of the cleanse - less headaches and migraines, less joint pain, losing some extra pounds (which are easier to maintain), better sleep, more energy and vitality, less allergic reactions.

If your case is severe (high level of toxicity), you can continue the detox period with fruits and vegetables, but make sure you consult with your physician and be under their supervision during this period!

The detoxing and healing power of juicing

We talked about cleansing with citrus fruit juices, but you can actually devise and experiment with all kinds of fruits, veggies, and roots. Some of them have extremely powerful detoxing and healing properties. They taste wonderful, tone the body, refresh and rejuvenate us. The thing to remember when preparing them is to choose fully ripe and well colored ingredients. It is best to have pure produce, free from GMO alterations, pesticides, and artificial fertilizers. Also try to use local seasonal fruits and vegetables. They are less likely to be treated with various chemicals to endure the long transportation, and they are more likely to had ripened under the sun (instead of a greenhouse), which stimulates the accumulation of beneficial nutrients. Remember that juices (without the pulp) quickly oxidize and rapidly lose their vitamins and nutrients. Try to consume the liquid within the first 5 to 15 minutes after preparation in order for you to take advantage of all its benefits.

How to decide which ingredients to pick? It depends on your personal preferences, but keep in mind that fruits are better at cleansing the body, while vegetables (the greens) are good for nourish the tissues and organs. So, they are both good and you can certainly try different combinations. Rotate the fruits and veggies (preferably by color) so that you can supply your body with different types of vitamins, nutrients, enzymes, and minerals. For example, roots (like beetroot) are excellent liver purifiers. Celery decalcifies harmful Calcium formations (like kidney stones, or creepers), and so on. In the next chapters we will explore various types of cleanses depending on the goal we would like to achieve.

You don't need to prepare any mixtures, if you do not wish. There is nothing wrong with choosing one particular fruit/vegetable and turn it into a healthy cleansing bomb.

If you want to make some sort of a detox mixture, the best bases are apples and carrots. They have gentle detoxing effects and pleasant taste. They are perfect for combinations with stronger purifiers like the leafy greens. For example, parsley (and other green spices and medicinal herbs) is full of strong essential oils, which can cause some unpleasant detox reaction in our bodies. Beetroots are also pretty powerful, and if taken alone in large dosages may cause a powerful healing crisis. Undiluted Celery juice in large quantities may harm our bones. So, the basic rule, when using strong healing juices, is to start small, incrementally increase their quantity, and dilute them in some apple or carrot juice. For example, start with one Tbsp. Celery juice diluted in four Tbsps. apple juice a day. In 2 days take 2 Tbsps. Celery with 3 Tbsps. apple. In two more days, add one more Tbsp. celery juice and combine it with 2 Tbsps. fresh apple juice. You can adjust the ratio according to your taste and tolerance.

Some combinations you can try are:
- o *apples and carrots;*
- o *apples and beetroot;*
- o *apples and cabbage;*
- o *carrots and cabbage;*
- o *carrots, spinach and parsley;*
- o *carrots, beetroot and cucumbers;*
- o *carrots, celery and parsley;*
- o *carrots, apples and beetroot, etc.*

Just experiment and see which ones appeal to your taste. Remember that beetroot juice is quite strong and you should start with small amounts (not more than 50 ml. a day). Later on in the following chapters we will further explore the power of these precious juice combinations.

For some great smoothie recipe ideas, check out Book 1 of the series.

What is the difference between juicing and smoothies?

Previously, I have mentioned the green smoothies and how we can add them in our daily or weekly detox plan. But what is the difference between an extracted juice from a fruit/vegetable/roots/green leaves and a smoothie? Which one is better? The short answer is they are both good for us, but for different occasions. The main difference is that smoothies contain all the fiber from the fresh produce, while juices do not have that. We all know how valuable fiber is. Even though we do not absorb it fully (unlike ruminants), we need these substances in order to stimulate the bowel movement and to take out our organic waste. Moreover, it slows down the absorption of the fruit sugar (fructose) and prevents from blood sugar spikes and insulin rushes. But if smoothies are so healthy, why bother with juices at all? Juices extracted from fruits, vegetables, roots, and leafy greens are also extremely beneficial for us. They deeply cleanse our cells, and have enormous healing powers. When we abstain from solid food for a definite period of time, our intestines are free to do one of their most important jobs – building our immunity. When we intake such juices, we give our bodies the needed nutrition (vitamins, enzymes, minerals), and let our immune system heal us at the same time.

A short recap:
Smoothies:
- o *Excellent for colon cleanses;*
- o *Fight constipation;*
- o *Prevent from various diseases;*
- o *Great energy suppliers (artificial energy boosters do not have any chance against a green smoothie!);*
- o *Keep their nutrients for longer periods of time;*
- o *Can be ingested more often.*

Juices:
- o *Excellent deep detoxifiers;*
- o *Have acute healing properties;*
- o *Refresh and tone the body;*
- o *Short expiration time - 5-15 min;*
- o *Should be taken carefully and in small dosages.*

Simple Ayurvedic Detox

This cleansing method uses one main traditional Ayurvedic ingredient – ghee butter. Before I describe the detox method with ghee, let me remind you of this not very popular clarified butter. The ancient Hindu wise men say that ghee is present in milk the same as God is present in their Creation. Nowadays this clarified butter is called *"the golden food"*. Until the present day, Indians still appreciate ghee for its culinary and religious functions. This butter is a key symbol for Indian culture for it's made of cow milk. Cow milk is a fundamental ingredient in ancient Hindu health, longevity, and wellbeing science of Ayurveda. According to the Indian culture, there are five main sacred substances (or divine nectars) – milk, yoghurt, sugar, honey, and ghee. You can find a combination of these ingredients in all sacred Hindu rituals.

Let's quickly recall how this precious detox substance is being prepared. Ghee is usually made of fresh unsalted cow milk butter. This butter is heated in special metal vessels on low temperature. As the butter begins to boil, it starts to froth. This foam is extracted without stirring the butter. Next, the remaining product simmers until it reaches a nice golden color and before it burns it is taken off the heat. After the butter cools down, it is strained with fine cheesecloth or muslin. Because of the processing, ghee does not become rancid and can be stored in a tightly closed container for a long period of time. Ancient wise men, the creators of Ayurveda, claim that ghee plays an essential part in keeping the balance between the human mind, body, and spirit. It keeps the three main elements in our bodies – vata, pitta, and kapha – in perfect harmony. This clarified butter contains a lot of essential fatty acids and the fat soluble vitamins (K, D, A, and E). Vitamin E and beta carotene are vital antioxidants which prevent from cell mutations, cardiovascular diseases, and diabetes. Modern medical science is finally beginning to understand and prove health principles which were discovered and practiced long ago by Ayurveda. Some of the benefits of ghee include improving eyesight, recovering from poisoning, strengthening the mental abilities and memory, toning the body and raising the vitality level. Some people even consider it as a potent aphrodisiac. Since this natural product has proven its many healing properties, the ministers in Hindu temples are passing the tradition and original ghee recipe from generation to generation.

Let's get to the detox procedure! This cleansing method also continues for 3 consecutive days (again preferably ending on the Full Moon). In the morning on an empty stomach just take some warm melted ghee. The aim is to bring the butter to the boiling point without burning it. If there is any foam on the top, remove it.

The amounts of ghee each day are as follows:
- *First day – **30 g (2 Tbsps.)***
- *Second day – **60 g (4 Tbsps.)***
- *Third day – **90 g (6 Tbsps.)***

After taking the butter, wait for about 30-40 min and start drinking pure warm water or tea (unsweetened). For lunch and dinner during the 3-day cleanse you can take boiled rice, preferably brown rice. Boil one cup of rice in 1 liter water without using any fat or salt. If you like, you can add some parsley or fennel.

If you experience any detoxing discomfort such as headaches, nausea, fatigue, take some honey and lemon juice diluted in some mineral water. If the cleansing symptoms are severe, stop the detoxing procedure and try it again during the next Full Moon.

The day after the cleanse is very important – in the morning take 1-2 Tbsps. Castor oil and 2 cups of tea. In an hour or two, you can have some fruits. For lunch and dinner, have something light – steamed vegetables are the perfect choice!

One day healing detox

This cleansing procedure can be executed when dealing with a cold or flu. All you need to do is take 50-70 g Epsom salt solved in some water in the morning on an empty stomach. This procedure will take a lot of fluids full of toxins out through the colon using reverse osmosis. Half an hour later, start drinking hot unsweetened tea or water. The total amount for the day should be at least 2 liters. You can take some lemon juice or honey, but try not to take any food until the next morning. This one day fasting can help the immune system take care of the virus on its own.

Monthly lung detox

Our lungs have been overloaded these days by smoking (active or passive) and breathing polluted air. Things are even more serious for people working in a dusty environment day in day out. Soon after the worrying symptoms begin – annoying morning cough, mucus coming out, inability to catch our breath, even the feeling of suffocation. If you experience one or more of these symptoms on a regular basis, pay close attention to this cleansing method. Also if you feel that the condition of your lungs has already severely deteriorated, consult with a physician first. This detoxing program can be beneficial for everyone, but you can always seek advice from your doctor. That is why in book 1 *"Healthy Body Cleanse: Gently Burn Body Fat and Lose Weight Naturally"* I paid special attention to how important it is to have a physician who supports the natural holistic medicine principles. But do not worry – the recipe is very simple and gentle:

1. Start the day with a freshly squeezed **lemon juice** (from 2 lemons). Dilute it in some water to make it more pleasant to drink. Drink this juice first thing in the morning on an empty stomach.

2. Between the breakfast and lunch prepare 300 ml **carrot juice**. For best results you can add up to 50 ml beetroot juice and some ginger.

3. **Tea for the lungs** – next we are going to make herbal infusion which is beneficial for the lungs. Mix equal quantities of oregano, plantain, peppermint, and lobelia. Next, take 2 Tbsps. of the herbal mixture and place it in 500 ml pure water. Bring the water to boil and take it off the heat. Let the herbs soak for at least 15 minutes. Now you can strain the infusion and drink twice a day during your lung detox. You can make a different herbal mix according to your preferences. Other herbs for the lungs you may consider are Watercress (Nasturtium officinale), Verbascum (Verbascum phlomoides) and Coltsfoot (Tussilago farfara).

4. During the lunch eat plenty of **Potassium rich foods** or drink a fresh green Potassium smoothie. The ingredients can be bananas, parsley, spinach, avocado, citruses, figs, tomatoes, apricots, etc.

5. During the day drink about 300 ml **pineapple or grapefruit juice** – it will further detox the body and expel more toxins from the lungs.

6. Before going to bed take a cup of **cranberry juice**. You can find an excellent cranberry immune booster and detoxifier in my FREE ebook *"10 Powerful Immune Boosting Recipes"*.

Go to mindbodyandspiritwellbeing.com/free-ebook and grab your copy!

7. Do regular **herbal or essential oil inhalations.** Just place a pot with some water in it on the stove. When it starts to evaporate put some Chamomile blossoms, or a few drops of Eucalyptus, Peppermint, Rosemary, or Thyme essential oils. Lean over the pot and cover you head with a towel so the hot air does not escape. Breathe deeply with your mouth open wide to reap all the benefits. This procedure can be done daily or when needed.

8. Also take frequent **hot baths** with Epsom salts, Bentonite clay, and essential oils to further detoxify the body. We have already explained these options in the weekly detox rituals.

9. Learn the **yoga breathing** techniques and apply them daily.

10. Make your own lung cleansing wine.

Here is the recipe:

Lung Cleansing & Healing wine

Ingredients:
   o 1 liter **bio wine** (aronia is a wonderful option);
   o 1 cup **dried or fresh herbs** (basil, coriander, dry chili peppers, parsley, dill, oregano, nasturtium, sage, rosemary, thyme, tarragon, etc. Try different combinations according to your taste.)
   o 2 **glass jars with screw lids**;
   o 1 **glass bottle**;

Directions:

If you use fresh herbs, wash them gently, let them dry completely, and cut them in smaller pieces. Mix the herbs well and divide them in 2 equal parts. Place each part in the jars. Pour about 500 ml wine in the jars, but don't fill them completely – leave some empty space at the top. Screw the lids and put the jars in a dry and cool place for at least a month.

After the time is up, strain the wine infusion with a fine strainer or cheesecloth. Pour the wine in the bottle (you may need to use a funnel) and the lung healing wine is ready for consumption.

Take in moderation – not more than 2 glasses for men and 1 glass for women per day.

3-day Lymphatic detox

Our lymphatic system is of great importance when it comes to our natural cleansing and healing processes. It is like the emergency squat that will counteract any virus or bacteria, disarm it and restore our natural healthy state. If the lymphatic system gets clogged, our abilities to fight diseases decline rapidly. If the situation is neglected, things get worse, you can even see and feel the lymphatic nodes getting swollen and painful (like the enlarged tonsils, for example). That is why it is so important to keep this system up and running like clockwork. Here is a 3-day cleanse specially targeted to assisting and boosting the lymphatic system and helping our bodies' defense system work effortlessly.

1. First of all, just like any other detoxing system, we need to **eliminate the toxins** that come in our temples as much as we can. Follow the guidelines in the first chapter, or if you need more help and a gentler approach, get book 1 and apply the simple tactics described there.

2. Drink lots of **Milk Thistle tea.** Take 1 cup boiling water and pour it onto 1 tsp. dry Milk Thistle fruits. Let it steep for 15 min and strain the infusion.

3. Combine this detoxing method with the **cleansing massages** from the previous chapters and pay extra attention to the lymphatic nodes – by massaging these special points we stimulate and purify the lymphatic fluid. You can also use dry brushing massages.

   Here is a list of the major lymph nodes that will guide you:

   o *Buccal node* – *it is located in the soft spots just below the cheekbones.*
   o *Parotid node* – *you can find it right at the beginning of the jaw right next to the ears.*
   o *Submandibular* – *the soft spot below the jawline.*
   o *Superficial cervical* – *below the ears.*
   o *Deep cervical* – *on the right and the left side of the neck.*
   o *Supraclavicular nodes* – *above the collarbones.*
   o *Infraclavicular* – *below the collarbones.*
   o *Axillary (Anterior and Lateral)* – *in the armpits.*

- o *Axillary (Central and Posterior)* – *below the collarbone where the arms meet the upper part of the breast.*
- o *Cubital nodes* – *in the elbow pit (called antecubital space).*
- o *Superficial and deep inguinal nodes* – *in the fold between the hip and the pubic area (just below the inguinal ligament).*
- o *Popliteal nodes* – *located in the knee pit (called popliteal fossa).*

4. Prepare this green **vegetable bullion**:

Take lots these veggies (preferably organic, not treated with chemicals): scallion, green peppers, zucchini, celery, spinach, parsley, cabbage, broccoli, lettuce, etc. Feel free to add carrots and beetroots, because of their countless nutrients and healing properties. Place the vegetables in a large pot and pour 9 liters of pure water in it. Seal the pot with the lid and let the plants simmer for 2 hours on low heat. After the time is up, take the soup off the stove and let it cool off. Next, strain the bullion and the lymphatic cleansing potion is ready. You can store the veggies in the fridge for later consumption.

Take this healing soup according to the following scheme:

Day 1: after you have prepared the bullion, you can take 1 cup (approx. 250 ml) of the liquid before breakfast and 1 more cup before dinner.

Day 2: take 3 cups of the bullion 3 times a day – before breakfast, lunch, and dinner.

Day 3: again take 3 cups of the liquid, but this time add the boiled vegetables as well.

Apple Cider Vinegar Detox

Apples are definitely one of the healthiest fruits known to mankind. All of the products made from them tend to have such beneficial effects on our wellbeing. One of these essential products is apple cider vinegar. Beside from seasoning our salads, this sour apple liquid can help us detox our bodies and improve our health. Here are some of the wonderful effects from taking even small daily amounts! ACV (apple cider vinegar) is known to lower the blood sugar level, it suppresses the abnormal high appetite and fights obesity, speeds the metabolism, cleanses the liver and gallbladder, takes out excess water (for people with gout), heals constipation, promotes the breaking down of kidney stones, supports the thyroid, fights hypertension and fungi, protects the blood vessels' walls (for people with varicose veins and hemorrhoids), etc. This natural elixir can also be applied externally for all kinds of skin issues (warts, skin tags, eczemas, etc.), for strengthening the hair and scalp, rheumatoid pains, muscle cramps, bone spurs, and so on.

Detoxing with ACV is very easy and it does not require much effort. Of course, to reach and preserve your healthy state you need to keep a proper diet and an exercise routine. ACV will merely speed and facilitate the process.

Here is what you need to do:

Take 1 Tbsp. raw organic unpasteurized ACV and dilute it in 1 cup of pure water. Take this mixture 2-3 times a day 20-30 minutes before a meal. Do not exceed the daily dosage and take it in short monthly detox courses. Do not use this cleansing method for a long period of time. ACV may draw out some essential minerals from the body if taken on a daily basis for a long period of time.

Important note: the fruit acid in apple cider vinegar can damage the teeth enamel. To prevent this, swish your mouth with water (or salty water) after each dosage. Do not brush the teeth, just rinse it!

ANNUAL DETOX

RITUALS

Annual Detox Rituals

*I*n this chapter you will find lots of cleansing procedures and detoxes, which can be applied on an annual basis. Of course, you can do them whenever you wish, but keep in mind that they are deep and extremely powerful. Prepare yourself properly, do not underestimate them, and do not apply them too often, or as a weight loss diet. Most of these methods are much more powerful than meets the eye. Do your homework, prepare yourself mentally and physically. If you need to, consult with your physician for further guidance. There is a high chance some of these detox rituals could turn out to be too harsh for you. So, do not rush into deep cleansing before you feel fully ready to do so. Start with the ones that look the easiest and dip your toes in the water first. And remember to always listen to your body!

Fasten your seatbelts, because we start head on with one of the main sources of discomforts and illnesses that needs our undivided attention – the guts!

Deep cleansing of the colon

Purification of the colon with enemas
"*All diseases start from the gut*" says the father of Medicine, Hippocrates. And he is right. When the natural bowel movement is impaired, the whole body suffers. That is

why in book 1 I started with some easy daily habits and tips to improve the work of this essential body area. This is the minimum basis so the colon and the intestines work properly and do their important job. Now it is time for some deeper and thorough cleansing. Every significant detox process starts with cleansing of the colon. Because what is the point of expelling waste and toxins from other parts of the body when the excretory systems are not working properly? The result would not be very pleasant – the unwanted substances remain in the colon and get reabsorbed back into the blood flow. No matter what kind of detoxes we do, if we do not start with the colon, the results would be miniscule, if any.

So, the easiest colon cleansing method is the enema. It may cause some controversy, but it is a well-known health procedure from the ancient times. Remember, this process is not intended to substitute a healthy diet with lots of fiber. Our intention is not to just evacuate the colon, because we have constipation. This cleanse aims to soak the intestines and expel any pathogenic debris, which cause us harm and illnesses. That is why I have put this detox procedure in the annual rituals. The enemas are not suitable for daily usage. We do not want to make the intestines lazy and unproductive. So, after we have got this clarification out of the way, we are ready to begin!

The only thing you will need is a suitable irrigator and a cleansing liquid of your choice. Choose an irrigator that would be the most comfortable for you – preferably with a long hose and a hook or a clip, so that you can put it on a high place. I will describe some options regarding the cleansing fluid. It is best to do this process at home when you are relaxed and when you have plenty of free time and a toilet at your disposal. You will also need some vegetable oil or some sort of balm handy for the irrigator's inlet.

Here is what you can use as a cleansing liquid:

- o **Salty water** – boil 2-3 liters of pure water and let it cool down at body temperature. Add sea or Himalayan salt – 2 Tbsps. for each liter water. Our goal is to prepare a salty saline, so when we insert it in the intestines it will suck out the waste by reverse osmosis. If the solution is not saltier than our physiological saline, this process won't work properly.

- o **Herbal infusion** – herbs are excellent for gently cleansing our intestines for their natural healing and disinfecting properties. Some good choices are St. John's Wort, Chamomile, Greater Celandine, etc.

- o **Lemon juice/Apple Cider Vinegar** – prepare the cleansing fluid by boiling 1 liter pure water and let it cool down until it becomes slightly warm. Next, add 2 Tbsps. lemon juice or organic apple cider vinegar.

- o **Weak Potassium Permanganate solution** – Potassium permanganate is a very strong compound, which has acute disinfecting properties. It is commonly used for treating problems with the urogenital system. Our goal is to make a weak solution so that we do not overdose with the substance. The Potassium permanganate must be between 0.01 to 0.1 % of the water amount. If you are not sure about the amount, take a close look at the color of the solution – it must be pale pinkish.

Keep it as pale as possible – this means the solution is weak.

- o *Honey water* – again boil 1 liter of pure water and when it cools off to body temperature, add 1 Tbsp. honey. This is a much gentler option on the intestines and the beneficial colon bacteria.

When you choose your desired cleansing liquid we can proceed with the method. It is best to prepare your body and mind beforehand. During the days before the detox procedure have light vegetarian meals with lots of fruits and vegetable fiber – this will make the process much easier. Also try to warm the body during this preparation period – have saunas, steam baths, soak in a hot tub, do the detoxing massages with the essential oils described in the previous chapters, warm the abdominal area with hot water bottle, use intense cardio training like running and dancing, etc. Do as many of these things as possible, if you are able to. This will dilate the blood vessels and soften the intestines' walls.

When the day of the cleanse arrives, it is time to evacuate the intestines – use laxatives of your choice or preparatory enemas. As I mentioned previously, the goal of the enema cleansing is to soak the intestines and flush out the harmful debris stuck on the colon walls.

This is the process itself step by step:

1. Fill the irrigator with the desired cleansing fluid and fix it at about 1 - 1.5 meters high.
2. Put some natural grease (vegetable oil or salve) on the inlet and the anus so that you do not harm the anal tissue.
3. Kneel on the ground and place your forearms on the floor, too. This is the best position for inserting the

cleansing fluid. If you are able to, you can try standing up, depending on the type of your irrigator.

4. Start slowly inserting the fluid, take short brakes if you need to. The exact quantity of the liquid depends on your personal assessment – at first it may be very small and as you get used to the procedure, it may be increased. Listen to your own body and do not put too much pressure on it, because we will be doing some yoga postures with the fluid inside the colon.

5. When you have inserted the cleansing fluid, lie in supine position on the floor (you can use your yoga mat). Keep your anal muscles tight and start slowly lifting your legs until you reach Candle position (Sarvangasana). Hold it for a couple of breaths and continue with Plow pose (Halasana). As you know, the colon has almost a rectangular shape. So, if we want to reach and cleanse all of its parts, we need to guide the fluid down its entire length.

6. Next, lie down again in supine position and turn on your right side for some time. This will move the liquid to the caecum.

7. Now lie down again for about 10-15 minutes to further soak the guts thoroughly. Do not worry if you cannot hold for a long time, you will be able to expand this period in time and practice. When you feel the urge to go to the toilet, evacuate the colon. If not, start doing your normal chores at home until you feel the urge.

8. Make 2-3 more enemas with the above described method. Remember that the more liquid you insert

the less time you will be able to hold it. When finishing the last round, try to evacuate the colon entirely. If you can't, add some more fluid until you will feel the urge.

In order for us to make this cleansing process complete and worthwhile, we need to do the enemas daily for a certain period of time as follows:

o *during the first week – **once a day;***
o *the second week – **every other day;***
o *third week – **once every 2 days;***
o *fourth week – **once in 3 days**.*
o *After that - once a week for 2-3 more weeks.*

Important: as I have already mentioned before, we don't use enemas to evacuate the colon and to deal with constipation. The aim is to soak the guts and dislodge any debris and polyps from the intestinal walls. Unfortunately during this process some of the beneficial colon bacteria are also flushed out. That is why enemas are not recommended for regular use, do this procedure once a year. And after the cleansing always replenish the colon flora with probiotics, prebiotics, bio kefir or Bulgarian yoghurt, pickles, apple cider vinegar, etc. For best results combine more than one method.

More information and recipes for replenishing the gut flora, check out book 3 of the series "Build Your Immune System Fast"

Shanka-prakshalana

This colon cleansing procedure is the Ayurvedic version of the enemas, but here the purification process happens throughout the whole digestive and gastro enteric system. That is why it works beneficially not only for the colon, but for our digestion, the pancreas, the liver, and intestines as well.

This cleanse, if done properly, can expel lots of toxins and old debris stuck in the intestines; it can improve our mood and energetic level; it boosts the immune system, improves the function of all internal organs; it stimulates not only our body, but our mind and spirit as well.

Do not apply Shanka-prakshalana if you are pregnant, or if you have any serious acute illnesses like dysentery, colitis, appendicitis, tuberculosis, diarrhea, colon cancer, stomach ulcer, etc. If you have any chronic illnesses or health conditions, consult with your physician first.

Ingredients:
- o 1 cup **salt** – *ground sea salt or Himalayan;*
- o *Several liters* **warm pure water** *at body temperature;*
- o *Some* **light vegan food** *(even if you are not vegan)*

Directions:
Choose a day when you are at home in a peaceful environment. It is best to be alone for at least 3-4 hours during the procedure. You need to be as calm as possible. If there is a pressing issue right now, choose another day when

you feel better and less stressed. We need our muscles and internal organs to be relaxed for the procedure.

The previous day you need to be properly prepared for Shanka-prakshalana. So, eat small portions of light vegan raw food – fruits and vegetables. Have a laxative (Epsom salt or herbal tea) for the colon to be fully evacuated in the morning.

Try to get up early the next morning during our natural cleansing hours – 6-7 AM. Warm some of the water so that it reaches body temperature. Dissolve 1 Tbsp. of the salt in 1 liter water and stir well. When the salt is completely dissolved, start applying the following schedule:

1. Drink 1 cup of the salty water.
2. Immediately after that start doing the following exercises without taking any breaks (if possible):

Shanka-prakshalana exercises:

- o **Exercises 1**: stand up with your legs wide apart at shoulder level. Extend your arms upward, and intertwine your hands while the palms are facing up. Keep you back straight, the arms stretched, and start tilting the body to the left and to the right. Don't make any stops until you make 4 tilts on both sides. Just like in the enema cleansing, here we are trying to guide the fluid to move into certain organs and body parts along the digestive system. That is how we will achieve a better and smoother cleansing procedure.
- o **Exercise 2:** don't change your position. While still standing up with legs wide apart, extend your right arm to the right horizontally. Next, bend the left arm and touch the right collarbone. Now twist the torso to the right as much as you can without moving your

hands. Ultimately you should be able to see your left heel. But at the beginning just try to twist and stretch as much as possible. Do the exercise on the other side, and make one more repetition on both sides.

○ ***Exercise 3:*** lie down in prone position and lift the body from the ground using your hands and toes. The legs are wide apart at about 20-30 cm. This position is very similar to the Upward facing dog asana. Now bend the torso to the right and back until you see the left heel. Don't hold or make any stops, immediately twist the torso to the left until you see your right heel. Make 4 reps on each side.

○ ***Exercise 4:*** if we managed to do the procedure correctly up to this moment, the salty solution must have reached the end of the intestines heading to the colon. So, the last exercise is designed to stimulate the evacuation of the fluid. Squat with your feet wide apart at 20-30 cm. Next, put your hands on your knees. Now twist the body slightly to the right and place the left knee in front of the right toes. Press the right thigh to the left flank, and twist the head to the right. Do it on the other side as well – twist the torso to the left, place the right knee in front of the left leg. Twist the head to the left and push the right thigh to the left flank.

If this exercise seems difficult to execute, you can substitute it with the `yoga Spinal twist (described in the liver detox asanas later in this volume).

3. Repeat the process in points 1. and 2. until you drink 6 glasses of salty water.

4. At this point you should have had urges to go to the toilet. If not, repeat the exercises until you feel the need to evacuate the colon.

5. After you go to the toilet, continue repeating the process in points 1. and 2. This time you may feel the urge to defecate with each glass of the cleansing fluid.

6. When you start flushing out clean water it is time to stop the procedure. Most people, who managed to finish the whole detox, report that this usually happens after about 14 glasses of salty water.

7. The final step is to drink a couple of glasses clean unsalted water and perform the so called therapeutic vomiting (Vamana). It cleanses the stomach and the esophagus from polyps, bacteria, and other harmful deposits.

8. If you feel any discomfort from all the liquid inside, repeat the exercises above until you feel better. Do an enema as a last resort.

Important note: do not leave the digestive system empty for a long period of time after this procedure! Half an hour after the process is over start taking some light foods. Do not wait to start eating more than an hour after the cleansing procedure. The most suitable dish after Shanka-prakshalana is Kitchari. If you missed the recipe, you can find it in the Ayurveda detox section. You can prepare a simpler version of the dish with only 3 ingredients – white rice, lentils and ghee. Take the same meal for the entire first day after the cleanse. The following days slowly start adding more products. Leave the meat and other animal products for later. Prepare light vegan meals, which are easy to digest. For example, steamed vegetables and cereal. Avoid some of the vegetables, which are high in hard fiber like broccoli and cabbage, they may cause some disturbance in the intestines.

The rule for replenishing the beneficial colon bacteria after the colon cleanse applies for Shanka-prakshalana as well.

Cleansing the colon with pectin

Pectin is a natural substance found in fruits and veggies. It is our natural cleansing assistant – it is highly absorbent and it can gently brush off food debris and toxins from the intestines without harming the beneficial bacteria. The best way to get more fiber and beneficial nutrients in our diet is to consume more fresh fruits and veggies, but that is not always possible (especially in the winter season). That is why we can find various pectin powder or liquid extracts that can assist us with detoxing and healing some gastrointestinal issues. Pectin is excellent at absorbing and taking out toxins and heavy metals; managing obesity and facilitating weight loss; it lowers the cholesterol level; prevents from blood sugar level spikes; heals constipation and colon irritation; supplies with the necessary fiber; lowers the negative impact from chemotherapy and radiotherapy, and more.

If you want a gentle but powerful natural detoxing method, apple pectin is an excellent choice. This cleansing technique is beneficial for anyone who wants to purify and stimulate their body, for smokers, people who regularly consume alcoholic beverages, those who fight obesity, high cholesterol; gastrointestinal issues (stomach acidity, colitis, gastritis, IBS, ulcers). Pectin is also useful for people who work under a lot of mental and nervous pressure and in a heavy metal toxic environment or near radioactivity.

The detoxing procedure is simple – follow the dosages of your pectin – liquid or powder. Just remember to take the pectin 30 minutes before a meal on an empty stomach and keep a proper diet. Choose the best quality product you can find, preferably extracted from apples (not citruses). The high quality bio pectin is basically harmless and it can be taken for long periods of time. I advise you to start small and see how your body reacts to this food additive. Listen to your body and if you feel fine you can make longer detoxing courses. After that, take a break and you can repeat the process annually. The key to achieving real long-term results is to make healthier changes in our diet and lifestyle.

Simple colon cleanse with flaxseed / linseed

Flax seed is an ancient crop which holds numerous benefits for us. Even the famous Indian natural medicine Ayurveda advises us to regularly use these small seeds (internally and externally) to improve various systems in our bodies – the respiratory system, cardiovascular system, eyesight, against infections, colds, the flu, rheumatism, fever, gout, etc. For this detoxing method you can use the regular dark flax seeds or the Golden ones, they both work well. The main difference is that the Golden flax seeds have softer skin than the darker ones. Either way you need to grind the seeds beforehand so that you can take full benefit of their detoxing ingredients. You can buy seeds on the market that had been ground beforehand, but I advise you to grind them at home so that they are fresh and full of their nutrients.

The colon cleansing method with flax seeds is very simple, but effective. It takes 3 weeks and some bio (homemade if possible) yogurt.

Here is the exact schedule:

a. **Week 1** – *take 1 Tbsp. freshly ground flax seeds daily in 100 ml yogurt.*

b. **Week 2** – *take 2 Tbsps. freshly ground flax seeds daily in 100 ml yogurt.*

c. **Week 3** – *take 3 Tbsps. freshly ground flax seeds daily in 150 ml yogurt.*

For best results you can grind and soak the seeds in some water the night before. They will absorb some of the water and bulk up forming their special mucus-like substance, which gently detoxes and heals the colon.

Some important guidelines:

o *During this detox drink plenty of water.*

o *Pregnant and breastfeeding women should avoid using this cleansing method – the lignans in the flax seeds contain phytoestrogen and can change the hormonal balance in the pregnant women's body.*

o *Insulin dependent diabetics should also be very careful when taking flax seeds on a regular basis. The seeds are high in fiber and they are proven to lower the blood sugar levels. If you have any related conditions consult with your physician before applying this detox method.*

o *Flax seeds also may slow down the coagulation of the blood. So, if you have such health problem or take blood thinners, you should be extremely careful with these little seeds.*

Flax seeds are praised by lots of naturopaths and conventional doctors for their numerous benefits. The Bulgarian specialist on natural medicine prof. Mermerski is one of those flax seeds supporters. In his book *"Healing and slowing down the aging process*" he states: "*Flax seeds are excellent for detoxing. They have the power to even take radionuclides and chemical substances out of our bodies.*" Here is one of his cleansing and healing (constipation and chronic colitis) recipes with flax seeds:

Take **2 Tbsps. flax seeds** and grind them (or crush them with mortar and pestle). Pour **1 cup hot water** on the seeds. Let it sit for a couple of hours or overnight and strain it. Take 100-150 ml of the mucus-like liquid 2-3 times a day.

For chronic constipation cases drink the flax seed mixture without straining it. Also add more fresh fruits and veggies to your diet.

Even if you don't have any health issues, you can use ground flax seeds for your daily fiber supply. The optimum amount is 1-2 Tbsps. a day. You can add them in soups, salads, smoothies, pancakes, mixed with yogurt or curd. One precaution, though – **do not exceed the daily dosage (25 grams) for long periods of time!**

Cleansing the liver

It is time to open up the heavy artillery! We continue our detox journey with one of the most important organs in our bodies. And when it comes to detoxing, we simply cannot go without it. I present to you, the workaholic of our organism, our waste treatment plant, the Mighty Liver! If the liver is cleansed and in a good healthy state, our overall wellbeing is pretty much ensured. But often, that is not the case. Our hectic lifestyles tend to put too much load on the liver it cannot handle. And the problems begin – chronic fatigue, moodiness, anxiety, depression, feeling sluggish, indigestion, hormonal imbalances, poor immunity, varicose veins, hemorrhoids (yes, they are connected like communicating vessels), etc. According to the ancient Chinese medicine, if we do not take care of the liver, we may head ourselves towards even more serious problems, like cancer. And it is logical – everyday thousands of cancer cells are being formed in our bodies, but our immune system easily takes care of them. But what happens when our natural detoxing and defense mechanisms are hindered? We know the answer...

We usually associate the problems with the liver with cirrhosis from regular alcohol consumption, hepatitis, or liver cancer. But these serious illnesses are only on the surface when the liver is severely compromised. When this important organ is not working to its optimum, it slows down its work, and we begin to experience various discomforts and even diseases, which we do not normally connect to the liver. This unhealthy state of the organ may even manifest as arthritis or heart problems. The reason for this is that we ingest far more toxic substances beside the alcohol and tobacco. The liver has the enormous task to filter every compound harmful for us – drugs and medications, artificial colorings and preservatives in food and drinks, even the vitamins from the pharmacy are not in their natural state and are usually being filtered by the liver. Do not forget about the stress overload. The regular stressful hormone secretion also loads and harms the liver.

Let's take a quick look at the various tasks the biggest internal organ constantly executes:

o *every single minute the liver filters about 2 liters blood from allergens, viruses, parasites, bacteria, and toxins;*

o *regulates the metabolism – transforms nutrients (proteins, carbohydrates, fats) into energy elements;*

o *produces enzymes for the proper digestion;*

o *breaks down estrogen – if the liver is clogged, the estrogen will accumulate and this may cause various issues like hot flushes, fibrosis, mastopathy, even breast/ovarian cancer;*

o *transforms valuable vitamins into their bioactive forms (A, D, E, K, B12), it also stores them in case of temporal deficiency (it keeps about a 4-month supply);*

o *it also keeps blood and glycogen in stock in case of an emergency. When our glucose supply is low, it converts some of the excess glucose to keep the blood sugar level high enough. And vice versa – when the blood sugar level is high, it stores the excess glucose and turns the remaining amount into fat.*

o *Creates a substance called the Glucose Tolerance factor. It works together with the insulin production to regulate the blood sugar level. When the liver fails to execute this function, we experience frequent fatigue and anxiety.*

o *Regulates the cholesterol level. The gall bladder in the liver produces the bile – liquid, which breaks down the fat, and excretes cholesterol. The bile also plays an important role in our detoxification by transporting the toxins from the liver to the intestines to be flushed out. Remember in the first book when we talked about the bile secretion and its laxative effect. It is a natural reflex to take out toxic substances.*

o *Builds our immunity. The liver plays an important part in our natural defense system along with the lymphatic system and the intestines. About half of the white blood cells in our bodies are located in the biggest internal organ (the liver). The so called Kupfer cells and the hepatocytes (two of the main types of liver cells) are the first filters for bacteria and toxic agents entering with the blood stream. Then, they produce specific enzymes, which transform the harmful agents into compounds that are easily disposed of in the urine or bile.*

The liver is truly a significant organ, which plays an essential role in almost every process in our bodies. It is no wonder that a compromised liver (congested, fattened or ill) may manifest in various symptoms, discomforts, or even diseases. I will list most of them, but I don't want you to become paranoid or hypochondriac. Just keep in mind that regular care for this precious organ is a must for our overall wellbeing. Here they are: a compromised liver may lead to chronic fatigue or sluggishness, especially after a meal; depression or frequent mood swings; frequent irritability, frustration, or even anger; PMS and reproductive hormone imbalances; digestive problems, or issues with the urinary tract; high cholesterol levels; chronic muscle and/or joint pain; allergies; acne, psoriasis, or any other type of skin problems; frequent blood sugar fluctuations; diagnosed fibromyalgia (constant pain in the muscles, joints, ligaments, etc.); high blood pressure; brain fog, poor concentration, or memory loss; issues with the intestines – frequent constipation or diarrhea; often feeling of nausea, or vomiting; swelling, bloating, and puffiness; problems with the metabolism (too fast or too slow), constant weight yo-yo effect; too sensitive stomach, chronic problems with indigestion, or heartburn.

Some surprising external symptoms of a compromised liver are: wrinkles between the eyebrows; constant bad taste in the mouth, or bad breath; dark circles under the eyes; unnatural unpleasant smell of the body; deposits on the tongue, etc.

A healthy and well-functioning liver can successfully filter most toxins, but in time, as it becomes clogged due to our unhealthy diet and high stress levels, it cannot do its job properly. So, the first sign is the skin. Remember some serious liver diseases are easily recognizable by the unnatural color of the skin such as jaundice. The same applies for stubborn acne, itching, and even psoriasis.

The compromised liver can also be recognized by our frequent bad mood, especially when we get frequently irritated over nothing. For example, in ancient Chinese medicine, when a person becomes too anxious, or depressive, they were given special herbs for toning and cleansing their liver. Also when a woman often experiences PMS symptoms, the first thing, which was treated, was the liver.

Another big tell-all sign that our biggest internal organ needs cleansing is the constant problematic metabolism, usually an extremely slow one. And it is logical – the liver controls the cholesterol and triglycerides accumulation, the blood sugar level, and if it's not working properly, we tend to store too much fat tissue and... hold your breath... we get CELLULITE!

As I have already mentioned, the liver is tightly connected to our immune system. So, if you frequently suffer from colds, flus, sinusitis, infections, asthma, allergies, or if you constantly feel tired, pay extra attention to this essential organ and take some steps towards its better functioning.

Another important connection to the liver is the work of the thyroid gland. Nowadays more and more people have a underactive thyroid. Maybe we can find the source where we haven't looked before. The liver regulates the thyroid hormones secretion, and transforms the thyroxin (T4) into the active triiodothyronine (T3). These hormones are responsible for the metabolic processes in our cells. But when the liver is compromised, the secretion and transformation of these compounds is hindered, and thus – our metabolism impaired. This may lead to uncontrolled weight loss or weight gain, rapid balding, issues with the blood sugar level, poor memory, severe mood swings, sluggishness, water retention (puffiness), frequent headaches and migraines, and more. So, if you are overweight (or too skinny), you have tried numerous diets without any success, maybe the root of the problem lies in a compromised liver.

But our physical body is not the only one that suffers from a congested liver. Ancient healing philosophies directly connect this organ to our emotional and mental health. As I already mentioned, in the traditional Chinese medicine, people with depression, anxiety, irritation, even with panic and fear, had been treated with liver cleansing procedures. In ancient Greece people also had been healing emotional problems by taking care of their biggest internal organ. Even the term "melancholy" means "black bile", which showcases the source of the problem. The explanation is simple – when we are stressed we produce special hormones, which prepare our bodies to respond to the threat (the "fight or flight" response). But to handle the stress properly, these hormones need to be processed and neutralized. And this job is again assigned to the liver. I told you this is the workaholic of our bodies! But what happens when this workaholic is overloaded with tasks? It cannot process all these chemicals and the stress hormones (adrenalin, cortisol) get stuck in the liver, and we lose our emotional balance as a consequence.

That is why I pay so much attention to this important internal organ. Improving its function creates a positive domino effect throughout the whole body. This is also the reason why most both ancient and modern holistic healing programs start by cleansing the liver (right after the colon cleansing).

So what are the first steps towards a healthy and well-functioning liver?
First of all let's take a quick look at some of the most common conditions and habits, which compromise and overload our precious organ: liver diseases (hepatitis, cirrhosis, etc.); regular consumption of alcohol; taking recreational or prescription drugs (steroids, oral contraceptives, antibiotics, even the artificial vitamins and minerals bought from the pharmacy); frequent exposure to toxic chemicals (pesticides, herbicides, fungicides, or other industrial compounds); problems with the bowel movement (especially constipation); too many parasites, bacteria, and/or fungi in the body; too much stress, or other strong negative emotions (especially if they are being bottled in); hypothyroidism (low secretion of thyroid hormones); indigestion; smoking (cigarettes, cigars, chewing tobacco, etc.). Try to eliminate the unhealthy habits you have as much as possible. Do not worry; this is not an

overnight wonder. It takes time, persistence and patience. Don't forget to consult with your physician about your prescription medications – are they absolutely necessary, or can you safely lower their dosages.

The next step is to start eliminating the foods, drinks, and other toxins, which load the liver. This may not be possible for you right away, but try to avoid them as much as possible at your own pace. You may want to check out the first book, which will provide you with lots of ideas, recipes, and strategies for the purpose of making healthier choices. Now let's take a look at the list! Avoid or stop ingesting altogether: refined white flour products; processed fats (trans fats); alcohol; refined white sugar products; fried food; highly processed milk from inhumane farms (milk coming from abused animals treated with hormones and antibiotics); fast food; carbonated drinks, and drinks with lots of artificial colorings, preservatives, and sweeteners. Also avoid overeating, and emotional eating. Include more fresh fruits and vegetables, fiber, and water in your diet. All this can happen in small incremental steps. If you have any current issue or diagnosed liver disease, you may be forced to make the changes much quicker. Consult with your physician for the full list of dietary do's and don'ts for your particular case.

Here are some more helpful pieces of advice, which will start your gentle liver detox before you move to the deeper cleanse:

1. Drink more clean water. The optimum amount is 30 ml per 1 kg of weight. If this is too much, incrementally increase your daily amounts according to your needs.

2. Drink a glass of hot water/tea with lemon juice first thing in the morning. This will stimulate the secretion of bile and it will help with the purification of the liver. Plus it works as a gentle laxative.

3. Start weaning off caffeine and replace it with healthier options.

4. Increase the consumption of leafy greens, especially the ones with bitter taste (dandelion, rocket salad (arugula), green mustard, chicory, dark green lettuce, etc.). The bitter taste of the vegetables stimulates the secretion of bile, which helps with the cleansing process. If you want to enhance their power, add some extra virgin olive oil and some freshly squeezed lemon juice.

5. Add vegetables and roots, which further help the work of the liver, in your diet. The best ones are beetroots, carrots, cabbage, broccoli, Brussels sprouts, and so on.

6. Include more fresh green herbs (the so called "medicinal" herbs) like parsley, basil, mint, rosemary, fennel, etc.

7. Not all fats are detrimental for the liver. Actually it needs natural fatty acids and Omega-3 and Omega-6 for its proper function. So, frequently use cold pressed (virgin) oils like flaxseed oil, sunflower oil, olive oil, hemp oil, borage oil, etc. Don't forget about avocados! They are full of such good fatty acids and they are an excellent addition to any healthy lifestyle!

8. Exercise regularly, or walk daily for at least half an hour. Later in this chapter you will find some specific yoga poses for stimulating the liver.

9. Relax, meditate, and release stress in any way you can. Realize that nothing is more important than your health and wellbeing. If you are not feeling well, you limit your ability to solve problems and to progress. Besides, when you relax and unwind, you may find that more and more ideas and solutions flow to you!

10. Gently massage and warm the area of the liver during the liver detox, or any time you feel like doing so. Use pure carrier oils and add some of the detoxing essential oils described in the previous chapters.

This elimination process can be long and difficult, but it is definitely worthwhile. That is why I wrote *"Healthy Body Cleanse: Gently Burn Body Fat and Lose Weight Naturally"* to help you in this process. You will find ideas for healthier caffeine, sugar and white flour substitutes, the best types of pure healing water, daily tactics and tricks to start expelling toxins, yoga poses for stimulating the cleansing process and speeding the metabolism, and much more.

Don't rush and expect everything to happen overnight. We have accumulated so much toxicity over the years, and it is not reasonable, nor healthy to try to detox everything for a month.

The good part is that if we manage to incorporate more healthy habits, we will be able to regenerate the liver and its proper function. Even the tiniest changes in our lifestyle practiced for a long period of time can make a massive difference. It is no coincidence that most cultures include cleansing procedures in their rituals (like the fasting period before Easter).

Here I will list some example recipes for boosting and cleansing this precious and important organ in our bodies:

Recipe 1

Ingredients:

- o *1 large grapefruit;*
- o *2 lemons;*
- o *300 ml pure water (distilled, filtered, mineral);*
- o *1 Tbsp. virgin flaxseed oil;*
- o *1 clove garlic;*
- o *A small piece of ginger root (about 2-3 cm);*
- o *A pinch of cayenne pepper (optional).*

These are the daily quantities. The cleanse lasts for two days, but prepare each batch right before consumption.

Preparation:

1. Squeeze the juice from the grapefruit and the lemons.
2. If you have a juicer, extract the juice from the garlic and ginger, too. If you don't, mince them well and press hard until the juice flows out.
3. Put the juices, the water, and the flaxseed oil in a blender and mix them for about half a minute. You can add more ginger and garlic if you like their taste.
4. Add the cayenne pepper if you wish, it is optional.

All of these ingredients stimulate the purification of the liver without putting too much stress and tension on it. The only downside of this recipe is the unpleasant smell of garlic. If the grapefruit juice didn't manage to soften its smell, take some parsley and chew it well. Or you can make this detox procedure in the weekend (or any other spare day) when you are not obliged to meet with people.

Try to exercise something light and refreshing during the day. Later in this book you will find out some yoga poses for the liver, which are excellent for cleansing days like this one.

Important note: before any liver detox take a week or two to prepare the organ for the cleanse. Eat light meals, and eat lots of sour fruits and veggies (sour green apples are an excellent choice). The sour substances stimulate the bile production and start the process of the liver detox. When the real cleansing begins, the organ will be prepared and the process will run much more smoothly.

The day after the cleansing, it is important to have a regular bowel movement. If not, do your best to evacuate the colon – with a laxative or enema. If we managed to start the cleansing process properly, the liver will dispose from small stone-like objects. They usually look like small soft green beans. These pieces are the waste, which clog the liver. That is why we need to flush them out ASAP. If they stay in the intestines for a long time, they will be reabsorbed, and our efforts will be futile. Do not worry, with each liver cleanse there will be fewer and fewer of them. But if you want to help the cleansing process even further, you can begin to take a large amount of apples or apple juice 3-4 days before the detox. The sourness of the fruit juice stimulates the bile secretion and promotes the successful cleansing process.

Recipe 2, variation I

Ingredients:

- o *1 glass of freshly squeezed* **citrus juice** *(from oranges, grapefruits, tangerines, lemons, etc.). The sourer the better!*
- o *2 cloves of* **garlic;**
- o *a small piece of* **ginger;**
- o *1 Tbsp. of* **virgin olive oil;**
- o *2 cups* **dandelion tea.**

These are the daily quantities. The cleanse lasts for 5 consecutive days.

Preparation:

Mix all ingredients (except the tea) in a blender and drink it immediately. Next, take the dandelion tea.

It is best to do this in the morning on an empty stomach at least an hour before breakfast. Don't forget about the bowel movement we talked about!

You can apply the detox 4 times a year, twice a year, or any time you feel you need a liver cleanse.

Recipe 2, variation II

Ingredients:

- o *1-2 freshly squeezed **lemons**;*
- o *1 cup **apple juice**, also freshly squeezed;*
- o *1 cup pure **water**;*
- o *1 clove **garlic**;*
- o *a small piece of **ginger root**;*
- o *1 Tbsp. **virgin olive oil**;*

Preparation:

Put all ingredients in a blender and mix them well for a couple of seconds. Drink the cleansing potion immediately. Take this in the morning on an empty stomach for 3-5 consecutive days. During these days have light vegetarian meals and try to follow the guidelines for the healthy liver I mentioned before. Avoid alcohol, and caffeinated drinks as much as possible. Don't forget to hydrate yourself properly!

Be aware that all kinds of cleansing procedures may cause some temporal unpleasant symptoms, like headaches, fatigue, irritability, itching, etc. These will end soon and they will be replaced with positive ones, such as feelings of lightness, joy, vitality, and so on. Be patient and persistent.

Recipe 3, variation I

Ingredients:

- o 1 cup **extra virgin olive oil**;
- o 4 Tbsps. of **Epsom salt**;
- o 3 cups **pure water**;
- o 3 cups of **fresh grapefruit juice**;
- o a bunch of **fresh grapes**;

Preparation:

Start the day with light vegetarian meals – fresh fruits and veggies. Stop intaking food at about 4 hours before the cleansing procedure, for example 15:00 PM.

At 19:00 PM start preparing the detox mixture. Combine the Epsom salt with the water and add the grapefruit juice. Divide this potion into 4 parts in 4 glasses. Start drinking the first glass immediately (19:00 PM). In two hours (21:00 PM) take the second cup. In two more hours (23:00 PM) squeeze the grapes in a cup, add the olive oil, and stir well. Drink this mixture and go to bed. You can adjust the time according to your schedule.

The next day, as you get up, take the third cup of Epsom salt and grapefruit juice in the morning on an empty stomach. In two hours, take the last cup of the mixture. After 14:00 PM continue the detox with some fruits and vegetables for the day.

This cleansing recipe is best to be applied during the weekend or other free days you have, because the Epsom salt is a strong laxative and it will cause some discomforts. But this is a needed step since we want to dispose of the liver "stones" ASAP, so that they do not get stuck in the intestines.

Recipe 3, variation II

Ingredients:

- o *750 ml **pure water;***
- o *4 Tbsps. **Epsom salt;***
- o *1 **grapefruit;***
- o *Half a cup **extra virgin olive oil.***

Preparation:

For this cleanse it is also advisable to start properly preparing the liver for the detox. Five days beforehand (for example from Monday to Friday) start having light vegetarian meals (preferably fresh fruits and vegetables). Avoid meat, dairy products, eggs, sugar, processed foods, alcohol, caffeine, etc. You know the drill! Have about 1 liter a day freshly squeezed apple juice (sour apples are the best choice). If it is difficult for you to find sour apples, substitute it with organic apple cider vinegar (1 cup warm pure water mixed with 1-2 Tbsps. ACV). Also avoid taking artificial vitamins, food additives, cold liquids, or medications (except the ones, which are mandatory for your health).

On the sixth day (Saturday) evacuate the colon thoroughly (with an enema or a laxative). At lunch prepare something light, such as brown rice with tomatoes and some salt. From 14:00 PM stop taking any food and drink only pure lukewarm water. Next, mix the water with the Epson salt and divide it into 4 parts. At 18:00 PM take the first part, and at 20:00 PM – the second one. At about 21:45 PM extract the juice from the grapefruit and mix it with the olive oil. At 22:00 PM drink the mixture and go to bed. You can adjust the time according to your schedule.

Just to remind you that the Epsom salt will cause quick and complete colon evacuation.

Recipe 4

This recipe is developed by the naturopath Dr. Yuri Kamenev. Yuri Kamenev besides from being a physician-naturopath is also a docent, Colonel of the Medical Service, and the author of more than 60 articles and several books dedicated to natural healing therapies. Here is a simple recipe for cleansing the liver he advises us to take once or several times a year according to our needs.

Ingredients:
- *150 grams **fresh cabbage;***
- ***Lemon juice** freshly squeezed from 1 lemon;*
- *Several **broccoli florets;***
- *25 grams diced **celery stalks;***
- *1 **pear;***
- *1 tsp. grated **ginger root;***
- *1 tsp. **turmeric;***
- *A pinch of **black pepper;***
- *500 ml pure or boiled **water;***
- *Several **fresh mint leaves**.*

Preparation:
Put the cabbage, broccoli, pear, celery, and ginger in a blender and start pureeing them as you slowly add the water. Next, add the lemon juice, the turmeric and the black pepper.

Take this detoxing juice once every other day for 2 weeks. After that, rest for one week and repeat the process.

Recipe 5

Full purification of the liver with olive oil and lemons

Ingredients:

- o *10-15 kilos **green sour apples** ;*
- o *2-3 kilos **beetroot**;*
- o *300 ml **lemon or grapefruit juice**;*
- o ***olive oil** or other type of cold pressed oil;*
- o ***cabbage and carrots** for 1 salad;*
- o ***Epsom salt** (optional laxative).*

Preparation:

This liver detox is extremely powerful and effective and it is vital to start this cleansing process with some preparation. Don't skip this step, because it is necessary to complete the detox properly and with less negative effects and complications.

Start having light vegetarian meals (preferably with raw fruits and vegetables) at least 2 weeks before the cleanse. Follow the guidelines for a healthy liver – no alcohol, unnecessary drugs, artificial vitamins, food additives, processed foods, caffeinated drinks, carbonated drinks, sugar, etc. It is not a good idea to overload the liver and all of a sudden to stress it out with a deep cleanse.

After the 2 weeks are over continue with this regime, but include 2 liters of sour green apples and beetroot juice. This quantity is the daily dosage, so drink this freshly squeezed liquid mix throughout the day (for example 400 ml 5 times a day). Don't rush –

drink consciously, slowly in small gulps. We already talked about the significance of the fruit acid in apples – it gently stimulates the bile production, dilates the liver canals, and prepares the organ for the cleanse. Don't forget to rinse your mouth after the juice, because it may cause tooth sensitivity and harmed enamel. This rule also applies for all citrus fruits and vinegar.

The apple juice preparation lasts for 5 days. During that time, try to include more warm water in your diet. It will further expel the toxins coming from the liver and gallbladder. Avoid cold drinks and foods, they will shrink the blood vessels and canals of the organs, and our goal is exactly the opposite. Try to abstain from meat, dairy products, and highly processed foods at least for these preparatory 5 days. If you wish to further facilitate the cleansing process (with less negative detox symptoms), take 1 cup of warm water with honey in the morning and before bedtime. This will soften the unwanted liver "stones" and ease up their evacuation. Another thing you can do to stimulate this process and prepare the liver is to take 1 Tbsp. fresh lemon juice with 1 Tbsp. extra virgin olive oil first thing in the morning.

It is also advisable to start doing some exercises to help with the process. Later on I will describe some yoga poses, which are excellent for liver cleansing, but you can do any type of movement you like. Keep in mind that cardio and aerobic exercises may be of great help with dislodging the liver stones. Also remember that strong negative emotions load this precious organ, so try to stay calm as much as possible, have enough rest and sleep. This is one of the best therapies we can do for our bodies.

On the sixth day, just before the start of the actual cleansing, it is best to evacuate the colon. Use a laxative of your choice or do an enema. The intestines must be prepared to expel the waste from the liver, so that no residue remains stuck on the way out. Next, drink a large quantity of the sour apple juice. At about 14:00 PM have a light vegetarian meal (a salad with olive oil and lemon juice is perfect). After that, abstain from any food. Water is allowed. Start warming the area of the liver; we want to dilate the blood vessels and canals in the organ. Use a hot-water bag, an electric pillow warmer, or anything of the sort. At about 16:00-17:00 make an enema again (or drink an Epsom salt solution, laxative tea, etc.), to be sure the excretory system is clear. Whatever method you choose, keep in mind that it has to take effect before 17:00 PM. Next, continue warming the liver. At about 18:00-19:00 PM squeeze some lemon juice (200-300 ml), mix it with the same amount of olive oil, and slightly heat it to body temperature in a double boiler. If you do not tolerate or do not like the taste of olive oil (extra virgin olive oil can have a slightly bitter taste), you can substitute it with another type of cold pressed oil. For example, oils from sunflower seeds, pumpkin seeds, sesame seeds, flaxseeds, hemp, etc. You can experiment and find your most favorable one. You can also substitute the lemons with grapefruits, they work equally well.

At 19:00 PM start drinking the mixture slowly in small sips. After you finish the liquid, lie down and continue heating the liver. You can stay in this lying position, or you can do some breathing exercises to help you further gently stimulate the blood flow. Sit on your legs and press your left nostril (you can plug it with a cotton ball, so you can be hands-free), and start breathing through the right one. As you breathe try to engage the diaphragm without moving your chest (try the diaphragm breathing technique). You can even put a pinch of cayenne pepper on the tongue to further stimulate the liver and the gallbladder in the detox process.

Go to bed according to your schedule, but keep in mind that you may wake up during the night with nausea, vomiting or diarrhea. This is normal, but the more properly we follow the guidelines of this cleanse, the less negative effects we might experience. This is why I focus so much on daily healthy eating habits. If the liver is severely clogged and constantly overburdened, this detox procedure may not be very pleasant. The more we take care of our bodies, and gently cleanse them, the less detox symptoms we have. So, keep the faith, and remember that despite the heavy rain (of liver stones) now, there will always be a rainbow in the end! These discomforts are more likely to occur between 01:00 and 03:00 AM when the liver is most active. Do not worry, it will pass soon. Again you can put some chili (cayenne pepper) on your tongue and breathe slowly with the diaphragm.

On the next day, get up early at about 06:00-07:00 AM. It is time to evacuate the colon and dispose of any trash, which had accumulated during the detox. Take the Epson salt or do several enemas to achieve

The Spirit Of An Indian Boy

Dustin Sommerio

I was only 11 or 12 at the time when our stepdad took our mom, my brother, Randy, and I to Yellowstone National Park. As a kid, you kind of dread long road trips, but this particular one was nice for me, as others had been, but this one is my favorite. So, after hours and days of driving, we finally arrived in Wyoming, such a beautiful and relaxing state. I remember us driving up one road as a vast buffalo walked beside us in traffic. I didn't notice until we started to slow down and our stepdad told us to look to our left, and there it was, a huge beautiful buffalo in its own home. It was magical to witness. If that wasn't cool enough, we continued our trip to a cabin rental place where we rented a little log cabin for the night. This is where our story really takes off.

I walked around this old, small log cabin, and started to feel at home. I set up a cot to sleep on that was on the left side of the room. My brother, stepdad, and Mom had the two beds that were on the right side of the wall and stuck out into the walk area. There was a small hall that dead-ended and turned to the left to a small bathroom.

Since we were all set up, Randy and I decided to go explore. If you know me and wonder why I love moose so much this is where my heart stopped in amazement. I walked to the back of the cabin where a moose stood and looked back at me. It couldn't have been more than 15 to 20 feet away. As I stared at this animal, it started to give a low growl to warn me not to get to close. I heeded the warning and went back into the cabin. I could hear my brother outside shooing away the moose. Randy was always a protective brother.

Night fell upon Yellowstone, and we all headed to our beds. I was exhausted from travel, so when I hit the cot I was knocked out fast. When Mom awoke to go to the bathroom at 2:30 AM, she rolled over to see a little Indian boy walk along my brother's legs, balancing like he was walking a tightrope. When the spirit got to Randy's chest, it jumped up and down, and every time it did Randy, still sleeping, let out a hard exhale.

From what Mom could tell, the Indian boy didn't mean any harm. He just wanted to play as he did back in life. As the ghost continued to play, our mother got worried that if he was causing Randy to exhale hard like this what else could he do. So, Mom walked toward Randy and the little Indian boy ran down my brother's legs and toward my cot where I was sound asleep. Mom then saw it cut down the small hall and into the dead-end wall where it disappeared.

When we awoke, Mom told us about the little ghost Indian boy and how she thought it was more exciting instead of scary. She said it was a haunting experience. It wasn't like the TV shows that overact and claim it was a demon, but rather it was more like how a family member has come back to reassure us that everything will be all right.

Today, I am part of a paranormal team in Illinois to try and witness my first ghost. Although I haven't yet seen one, I still hold out hope one day my experience will be that of like my mother's.

The Whammy At Cheney Mansion

Mike Ricksecker

The beautiful Victorian Cheney Mansion began its existence as the much more simplistic "Red House," the first frame house ever build in Jerseyville, Illinois, then known as Hickory Grove. Built in 1827, the Red House was a tavern and stage coach station by James Faulkner along what was known as the old "State Trail" between Jacksonville and Alton. It was just a few years later that Faulkner sold the Red House, and in 1839 it was sold again to Dr. E. A. D'Arcy whose daughter married Prentiss D. Cheney. It was Cheney who built up the mansion as it is seen today and incorporated the original Red House into its construction.

There were a number of P.D. Cheney's over the years, the last which was a drunk and is well known as one of the resident ghosts of the house. He was well-educated and a fine musician, but his first love was the military, even though he never served. The uniform he is pictured in on a wall in the house was handmade, not issued, and he wore it as often as he could. P.D.'s behavior was deemed eccentric, at best, with scores of stories floating around town about the mischief and mayhem from his drinking binges. One story includes him reeking so bad in his uniform at the bar that some of the locals dunked him in a horse trough. His wife divorced him, but he remained at the mansion, his wealth in no real trouble. And he is still there, long after he's been deceased.

Shana and I first conducted a paranormal investigation of the Cheney Mansion as guests of Ron Turner of Paranormal free Agents. It was a fantastic treat for my birthday, and they even surprised me with a cake that night. The tour of the historic mansion given by Ron and Mike Pedersen was fantastic, and gave us a thorough introduction to the history and spirits of the old home. If you're ever in the area, I highly recommend at least a visit for a tour, including a recreation of hickory Grove by the county historical society. Hostess Carol Senger was extremely gracious and kind, and new friend Karen Whitaker joined us for the investigation. All-in-all, the ghosts of the Cheney were rather on the quiet side for us that first evening, although we did discover a "lost" local cemetery while sifting through old maps of the town. But that adventure is another story for another time.

To say P.D. Cheney doesn't care much for other men roaming about his quarters is probably an understatement, and the second time Shana and I investigated the mansion I learned that very lesson. P.D.'s bedroom is on the second floor, the first on the left as you come up the stairs. Technically, there is another room off the stairs as you ascend, a bedroom for the servants on the half floor between the first and the second since servants weren't allowed to sleep on the same level as the masters of the home. But P.D.'s room is the direct left at the very top of the stairs, and it is very much his domain as he is wont to let men know.

P.D. Cheney "in uniform."

Shana and I formally introduce ourselves whenever we begin an investigation in any room. That particular evening, we'd already spent some time in the doctor's office on the first floor and the children's room (former servant's quarters) on the half floor, so we were systematically working our way up the building, reacquainting ourselves with the spirits of the mansion along the way. Perhaps, P.D. wasn't home the first time we investigated, because he was sure there the second time, putting "the whammy" on me, as Carol later said.

I don't claim to be psychic, but I do have "sensitivities" to the paranormal, and this night I was extra sensitive of P.D. Shana and I were making our routine introductions, "Hi, P.D. I'm Mike, this is Shana. It's a pleasure to meet you," when my head started throbbing. It wasn't a standard headache but some sort of strange pressure that was squeezing my skull. We continued with the pleasantries for several minutes, but I had to sit down. While I sat, the pressure mounted, and Shana handed me a sizable piece of black tourmaline crystal to try and help the situation. Black tourmaline is supposed to help block negative energy and transform dense energy into a lighter vibration. It wasn't helping.

I continued to sit in the chair, one hand clenching my head, the other holding the stone while the pressure persisted. Suddenly, a light crack emanated from my hand holding the stone. My eyes shot to my fist, which wasn't clasping the black tourmaline very tightly, and the crack sounded again. I alerted Shana to what was going on and handed the stone back to her. We decided that was a good time to take a break.

Downstairs, we freshened up with dark chocolate and water, a needed respite since we'd been at it for a couple hours. I also freshened up in the restroom, but when I came back, Shana had her hands outstretched, a piece of the tourmaline in each palm. "It broke in half!" she exclaimed.

Black tourmaline is considered a hard stone, measuring 7.0 – 7.5 on the Mohs scale. To put it into perspective, quartz usually measures at about 7.0, and the hardest diamonds measure at a 10. In other words, I may be strong, but I'm probably not going to be crushing hard crystals with my bare hands. Yet, here was this black tourmaline split in two.

Suddenly, we heard movement and a moan emanate from the monitor set up on a table in the second-floor hall. The Cheney Mansion is wired with security cameras and audio monitors throughout the house. These can all be watched and listened to from the break room (the rear sunroom) of the house, and it's what Carol does while paranormal teams investigate the mansion. She has frequently witnessed paranormal activity on the displays.

P.D.'s bedroom on the second floor.

We all glanced up at the monitor, and Carol told us precisely where it came: "Upstairs in the middle of the hall after you pass P.D.'s room."

I pivoted and looked up at the ceiling. "I'm going to check it out."

Up I went, right back into the fire. I wasn't headed into P.D.'s room this time; I was just headed to the hallway, even if it was just outside his quarters – at least that's what told myself. While P.D. room's is at the top of the stairs to the left, the short balcony hall makes an immediate right and wraps around to three other rooms of the level. Also, straight from the stairs is a small sewing room with a locked entrance to the tower of the mansion. The table on which the monitor sits rests between the sewing room and what is know as "Miss Dorothy's" room, the next room on the left as you walk the horseshoe.

I stood in front of the table and glanced about, but didn't see anyone. "Hello? Is there someone up here? We heard you downstairs."

Place of refuge: The sewing room.

Suddenly, a sharp pain pierced my right shoulder as if someone was stabbing me in the back of my shoulder blade with a sharp object. "Ow! Hey, you're not allowed to do that!"

Over the years, I've heard plenty of stories from other investigators about how they've been scratched or injured by something unseen, the most alarming always being those that produce scratches of three lines, the theory being that the entity is mocking the Holy Trinity. In all of my years of investigating, I've never had that happen, nor have I ever sought to have it happen. The most physical any entity has ever gotten with me was the one that almost made me pass out in the library of the Stone Lion Inn in Guthrie, Oklahoma. After being involved with the paranormal in some way, shape, or form for more than 25 years, it flashed in my mind that this could be my first "injury."

I spun about and slipped into the sewing room, repeating that the spirit was not allowed to touch me like that, that we were just interested in learning more about the house and the people that lived there. Inside the sewing room, the pain in my shoulder blade subsided. When it felt like the moment had passed I stepped back out into the hall, performed a quick sweep of the second floor, and returned to break room to join back up with Shana and continue our investigation that evening.

The Cheney Mansion and its haunts are extremely charming and are an authentic glimpse into frontier life in that part of Illinois. The house has been beautifully restored, with scores of artifacts and antiques, some original to the house and others unique to the time period. The mansion even includes a hidden room, accessible now through the basement, that was used by the Underground Railroad and featured a trap door from which food was lowered to slaves on the move from the South.

Whatever you may be looking for in a historic haunted house, the Cheney Mansion has it, including a resident ghost named P.D. that may just put the whammy on you.

Mike Ricksecker is the author of the historic paranormal books *Ghosts of Maryland* and *Ghosts and Legends of Oklahoma* and the hybrid paranormal research series *Ghostorian Case Files*. He has appeared on Animal Planet's *The Haunted* and Bio Channel's *My Ghost Story*, Fox 5 News (Washington DC) and Coast-to-Coast AM, and he produces his own Internet shows "Ghosts and Legends" and "Paranormal Roads" on Haunted Road Media's YouTube channel. Additionally, Mike is an Amazon best-selling mystery author with two entries to his Chase Michael DeBarlo private detective series, *Deadly Heirs* and *System of the Dead*. Visit his web site at: www.mikericksecker.com

Good Golly, Miss Molly

Shana Wankel

One of my favorite things about investigating a venue multiple times is the relationship that we sometimes develop with the spirits we come into contact. Society of the Haunted has investigated and explored Mineral Springs Hotel in historic Alton, Illinois, on numerous occasions, and we have never been disappointed in the outcome.

Last year, during one of our investigations in the upstairs area, we decided to spend some time in a room that we didn't routinely visit. We usually spent most of our time investigating the room where a spirit named Pearl resides. Her death is documented to have happened there, and since I had established actual physical and emotional contact with her, it made sense to focus on her. However, we decided to leave her room and make our way down the hall to another room.

The energy in this other room was quite literally creating a buzzing sensation in the atmosphere, and although this energy was strong, I didn't feel that it was dangerous or malevolent. We lingered for a bit, but eventually had to leave, paid our respects, and said goodbye.

When we reviewed our evidence, we discovered that someone in the room had said my name, and fortunately, were able to capture it on our audio recorder. As you can probably imagine, this new evidence made the room even more compelling to me. Who was it that said my name? Did Pearl decide to leave her room and follow me into a new room, or was it someone different?

In June 2018, Haunted Road Media had the privilege and honor of holding our first of many-to-come paranormal conventions inside the historic ballroom of Mineral Springs Hotel. As with most paranormal conventions, an investigation that was open to the public was conducted that night after the day's festivities. There were a large number of people participating in the investigation, which meant everyone would be milling about on all five floors of the venue. Because of the varying investigative styles involved, there weren't that many quiet moments of which to speak.

A small group of us made our way upstairs towards the room where the EVP of my name had been captured. It was a balmy night, and since we were on the top floor and heat rises, the temperature was a bit distracting. As an empath, sometimes outside forces such as uncomfortable temperatures will interfere with my concentration. The random device noises and chatter coming from other areas of the floor we were on was also a factor to contend with.

I started the usual line of questioning toward whomever was in the room with us and mentioned that I heard her or him call me by name on a previous visit. In between the questions, I was carrying on a conversation with the others in the room with me. I gradually started feeling the energy in the room change and felt it emanating strongly from the direction of the door. It felt like someone entered the room, and I was hoping to get a lockdown on their identity.

Sometimes in my mind, I'll sense a name or a letter that the name starts with. Other times, I'll actually get a vague glimpse of features. This particular time it was the letter "M" that flitted through my mind, and so, I asked if his or her name started with that letter. Immediately, the energy became stronger on my right side in between me and the door. I also experienced what felt like a human hand touching my right arm above my elbow. I put total concentration into exploring that energy and closed my eyes to focus on a name.

When I'm in "empath mode" and trying to make sense of certain energies, it requires a lot of effort. Inside my head, it sounds like several quiet conversations going on at the same time, and none of it is discernable. This time, though, I felt the name "Molly" quite strongly. I tentatively asked if the person in the room was named Molly. Almost immediately, the energy to my right grabbed my arm with enough force to really get my attention, and I jumped. With more conviction, I asked if Molly was his or her name, and the response was significantly stronger. In fact, it was strong enough to make me jump up and over to where Mike was sitting to my left. The wave of energy that swept through and around me made its way over to him, and he actually backed up from it.

Shana in Molly's Room with Zara the Zombie Doll.

The feelings that were barreling through me were electrifying and emotional all at once. The experience left me with a multitude of questions which I, sadly, didn't get to devote more time to during that investigation. The public investigation was still going on, and unfortunately, we needed to move on. I said my goodbyes to "Molly," Pearl, and another younger spirit in the area as we passed their rooms. Leaving Mineral Springs that night was more difficult due to the events of the night and the unanswered questions I had.

My next experience with Molly was a very emotional one and definitely merits further research into her existence. It's Raining Zen hosted an event one Saturday afternoon which allowed the public to create their own zombie dolls. The doll I chose to modify reminded me of the very first child spirit I ever saw and interacted with. While I was painting, I was also thinking of a name for her.

The letter "Z" struck a chord within me, and the name "Zara" came to mind.

After the event, Mike and I were given the privilege to investigate upstairs, and we went straight to Molly's room. I immediately felt her presence and started up with the usual banter. There were three chairs set up in the middle of the room. Mike and I each took a seat and put Zara on the chair in between us. We also put a K2 meter near Zara to attempt to capture telltale signs of approaching EMF energy.

A strange thing started happening during this time. I started to see what is best described as the shimmering effect that usually happens when heat energy from a fire rises up from the flames. This was taking place in between me and the chair where Zara was sitting. I'd never experienced this particular phenomenon before and wondered if this was energy coming from Molly. I asked Molly if she liked dolls and if she could see Zara. Shortly after, the energy in the room shifted, and a wave of sadness swept over and through me. It happened so fast. My throat started tightening up, and before I could stop it, I was crying. For a few moments, I cried as if my heart were breaking. Eventually, the feelings of sadness subsided and the energy became less strong.

After this experience, Mike and I discussed what had just happened. We feel that Zara was definitely a trigger object that day. Did Molly have a doll at one point in her life and was Zara a reminder of that? The events of that day in Molly's room, combined with previous interactions with her, makes us even more compelled to know her and delve into her past.

To this day, I still make it a point to visit and interact with "Molly." Further research will be done to try to find her origins and story. Was she a resident at the hotel or just a visitor passing through? Is her name truly Molly? Each visit with her brings new experiences to research and document. I feel strongly that my relationship with her will grow in the coming months, and I'll find the answers I seek regarding her identity.

The paranormal field is sometimes frustrating due to the lack of documentation of events. Another frustrating fact about being an empath is that while we trust our feelings, we cannot always trust the information that comes to us. It is not an exact science. Research and further exploration of these venues and the spirits we interact with are a MUST. I'm looking forward to unlocking the mystery of Molly.

Shana is a paranormal investigator with 10+ years of experience and enjoys the thrill of researching historical landmarks, venues, and the spirits that inhabit them. She's also an aspiring author and an Empath. She's a firm believer in showing spirits respect, keeping their memory alive, and reaching out to them in a way that makes them comfortable to interact. Shana recently joined forces with Mike Ricksecker and Society Of The Haunted, is an active member of Haunted Road Media, and is the Procurer of Music for Enigma Underground Radio.

Hellfire Club

Vanessa Hogle

I wasn't quite sure what to expect when I came within sight of the infamous "Hellfire" club, just outside of Dublin, Ireland. I knew what I had felt from photographs, but they paled in comparison to the real thing. I stood there, taking in the formidable construction, the absolute power it seemed to radiate. I realize that may sound like a romanticized description but nothing else does it justice. It was still quite cold in March and snow still clung to patches of grass and gravel making it difficult to navigate. This was exacerbated by the man I saw standing just outside of the building, to the back.

He was staring at me. Why, or how, I held his gaze still remains a mystery to me. I couldn't break the connection, repulsive as it was, and I didn't want to. My original intentions of going, immediately, into the building vanished as I made my way to an area to which he had turned his gaze. A large boulder sat on the outskirts of a mound, concave in the center, facing the back of the building. I sat down and did what I do best -- I sketched him.

Calmly he stood there, still as a statue, and let me hazard out a rough sketch of him. His tall, pointed, papal looking hat made it into the drawing but his robes would have to wait till I had more time. His face was cruel. His lip snarled without making a sound, and his eyes were like chunks of ice, the palest blue. What I could see of his hair had a similar hue due to the stark whiteness of it.

No sooner did I finish the sketch, he disappeared. Just like that. It didn't matter that no one else had seen him. I did. Clear as day, and I knew him disappearing was just his way of getting me inside the building without asking.

The infamous Hellfire Club.

Admittedly, my initial exploration of the rooms didn't bother me. They were benign, at best, and only held a small tremor of perceptible energy in them. It wasn't until I stepped into the room behind the stairs that my breath caught and my heart began to race.

There, in the corner, I saw a small girl. She couldn't have been more than four or five years old, if that. She was huddled with her head resting on her knees, anchored by scrawny little arms. She was naked and cold. I never saw her face. It was hidden by long, filthy hair of an indiscernible color. To her left, in front of a bucket I can only assume was used for private moments, lay a young man, maybe 10 years old, bleeding. His life was pooled underneath him, spreading out, and the backside of his malnourished body was covered in wounds. They had to be whip wounds as they crisscrossed his back and buttocks.

He was long gone. Why I saw him, I have yet to figure out. But the little girl's spirit felt "present." Granted, there was no communication with her. She never made a sound, but I have to believe she was showing me all this for a reason. That reason was partially confirmed when I realized the room we were in was at the back of the building... right where I had been sitting... right where the man had been standing. This was no coincidence. I may not have been able to get to the bottom of it then, but you can be damn sure I will when I go back.

Vanessa was practically born into the field of the paranormal, having her first experience before the tender age of two. Since then she has been a consultant for the "Leave or Die" episode on Animal Planet's show *The Haunted*, made numerous appearances on radio and YouTube shows like "Paranormal Zone TV," "Paranormal Connection," "Beyond The Strange," "Live Paranormal" and "Spaced Out Radio." She also co-hosts a successful YouTube show "Edge of the Rabbit Hole" with her publisher, and dear friend, Mike Ricksecker. Vanessa has published three books and has been featured in three more, all relaying her experiences in the paranormal. Her paranormal travels have taken her all over the United States, England and Scotland. In the last three years she has remote viewed, consulted for or investigated over 260 cases world-wide... with many more on the horizon.

You can learn more about Vanessa and what she does at her blog, hottamalered.blogspot.com.

I'm A Shadow Person...
Really!

Donna Gorton

I was once on a paranormal investigation at a Historical Society. While being given a tour of this beautiful old three-story building, the team I was investigating with were stopped on the second floor trying to get the DVD camera system set up.

I had just finished hearing the history of the building from the Director and was sitting on the first step of a flight of stairs leading down to the Main Street ground floor entrance. My team member was having difficulties getting the camera system up and running and was quickly getting frustrated. The building has air conditioning, but it had been shut off for the weekend, and it was a sweltering August summer night. I could tell his frustration level was quickly rising.

I should also mention that I'm a psychic medium. Before sitting on the step, I felt an energy down at the bottom of the stairs. What I "saw" down there was a large shadowy mass that was darker than the darkness. It would morph here and there taking on a subtle humanoid shape, but then quickly change back to the mass form. I tried communicating with it. There was no reply.

For me, this is unusual since I can usually still sense male or female and approximate age of a spirit even if they won't speak to me. But I got nothing! I tried introducing myself and the team, explaining why we were there, everything I could think of, and still it (I say "it" only because I still wasn't getting anything off of it one way or another) remained silent. I felt nothing threatening from it, which was good.

I watched my teammate growing more and more impatient over not getting the camera system online. He kept mumbling how he didn't understand since he had checked everything the night before, and it worked fine then. I suddenly had an "Aha!" moment and quietly asked whilst looking down at the undulating mass, "Are you messing with the equipment?"

I got a defiant, "Yeah!" back from it. So, I asked it politely to stop interfering with our machines.

As I was talking, I don't know if it let it's guard down a bit or what, but suddenly I knew it was a male, maybe in his early 30s, and not some unknown shadow mass entity.

I tried another tactic -- the direct approach! I said to him, "Ok, sir, I appreciate your honesty but don't understand why you're trying so hard to block me."

I heard his reply loudly, "I just want to be left alone!"

At this point, my tech guy's wife and fellow teammate had come to stand next to her husband wondering what was the hold up. She whipped her head around to me and said, "What?" loudly like she had been startled.

I told her I didn't say anything.

"But you heard that, right? What was that?"

I explained the interaction I'd just had and asked her to give me a second while I addressed the unknown male spirit.

I turned my attention back to him and this time he seemed to be staying in a humanoid shape. I think he was still trying to cloak his identity from me!

"Ok, I have a proposition for you, sir. We need our equipment to work and you want to be left alone. Please stop interfering with it, and I promise to not intentionally bother you again tonight. Deal?"

In response, the DVD system suddenly started working again.

I only ran into him two other times during our investigation, and both times I kept my word. The first was when he was trying to hide in an unused closet space, and I respectfully just closed the door after looking inside and seeing him. The last time was when I was being shown the massive basement by the Assistant Director.

He saw her with me and immediately tried resuming the shadow mass form. It seemed like we had startled him. I couldn't help but chuckle because it was as if he was trying to change form to be scary again like, "I *am* a shadow person! Really, I am!"

I merely whispered to him, "You're fine," and we kept walking.

Never before had I encountered a spirit trying so hard to be scary and failing!

Dark Attachment

Shawn Gilmore

When I was 13 years old, I lived in a condominium in Chagrin Falls, Ohio, with my mom and two sisters. The condo is in a large apartment building. The complex was two large buildings that are shaped like a "Y." Previously, the complex had been an adult-only community. We were actually the first family with kids to live in the buildings. We lived on the fourth floor which was also the top floor. Our condo was one of four of the largest units that were inside the building. The unit had three bedrooms and three and a half baths. My bedroom was the smallest of the three bedrooms. The full bathroom was across the hall from my room. Both of my sisters shared a bedroom which was next to mine. Their bedroom had a walk-in closet, and a bathroom attached to it with a stand up shower in it. My mom's room was a lot like my sisters' except it was larger and had access to the balcony. Between the bedrooms was the living room, dining area, tv room, and kitchen. The large unit had two entries. One entry was located by my bedroom and the other entry was by the kitchen and my mom's room. Right across the street from the condo was the Chagrin River and a park. The park was a large open field with a baseball diamond on the far back corner. There was a paved path going around the park with exercise stations placed throughout and a small playground in the other far corner that was across from the baseball field. This is all important because of all of the events that took place throughout my years living at this condominium.

When we first moved into the apartment, my sisters and I were just moving in with our mom for the first time since I was in kindergarten. Before that we lived with my grandparents. It was a new town and our family was broken and was trying to rebuild. To say it was a big change is huge understatement. I had high hopes for our new home and for our family. My sisters are twins and a year older than I. They hated everything about the move.

Things started off quiet. Every once in a while, I would feel like I was being watched while I was in the shower and while I was in bed. Sometimes I would hear noises coming from the kitchen. Then things started to disappear and move from one room to another. For example, I would place my house keys on the kitchen counter and then when I would go to get them they would be on the kitchen table or coffee table in the tv room. Then it escalated even more.

We would wake up to find that all of the cupboard doors had been opened. My mom would blame this on my sisters and I. My mom would also accuse us of cooking at 2:00 or 3:00 AM in the early morning when we had actually been sleeping.

When I was around 16 years old, my mom and I shared our experiences. She even shared with me that she spoke with one of our downstairs neighbors and she said weird things happen in her unit as well. It was at this time that my mom and I had both agreed that our home was haunted. My sisters didn't agree and said we were crazy.

That was as bad things got for a while. Then I came home one night and my sister and her friend were using a Ouija board in the stairwell of the building. It was a cheap kind like what you buy at a toy store. The stairwell is where we would smoke during the colder months or if it was raining outside. I tried to use the Ouija board too, but it didn't work for me, so I told them not to use the board inside our condo and went inside.

After this, every time this one friend of my sister came over they would use the Ouija board. On one separate occasion after this, I remember trying to use the board again and it didn't work this time either. I had my sister ask why it wouldn't work with me. It spelled out the words "too confused." After this, things got really intense.

One night, my sister and a group of her friends were talking in their room. My sisters and I had a lot of the same friends, so because we were all friends, I decided that I would join their conversation. My sister's friend was talking but her voice sounded weird. It didn't sound like her. My sister was acting weird, too. I thought they were joking around and trying to scare their other friends. I shouted that the eyes of a large stuffed Lion King plush toy looked real. To this day, my sister still claims she was "just joking around" throughout all of this.

After that night things changed. Instead of just feeling as though I was just being watched in my room, I felt like something or someone was standing over me and watching me everywhere. I couldn't look into a mirror in the condo without getting the chills or uneasy. When I was in the shower it felt like something was staring at me. It was at this time that I no longer felt comfortable sleeping in my bedroom.

During this time, I worked at a large retail store called Marc's. I would feel like I was being followed when I walked through the stockroom. One time while I was at work, I heard footsteps and no one else was around. After work one night, I got home and found my sister and her friend in the stairwell playing with the Ouija board again. I asked them to ask if whoever they are talking to through the board was the one who was following me and watching me. The planchette gave a response by moving to the word "Yes."

I then had my sister and her friend ask, "Why?"

It spelled out, "Challenge."

I didn't know what that meant. I only knew that I didn't like it.

By this time, I was sleeping on a couch in our living room almost every night. I started having violent dreams and felt too uncomfortable to get a good night's rest in my bedroom. At this point, things were also starting to disappear and not return, and it was always my favorite things that would disappear. For example, my favorite band t-shirts from concerts I had gone to and cash would mysteriously disappear without a trace. They were both things that I kept track of and never wanted to lose.

I finally got to the point where I wanted to do something about what was going on. I was brought up Jewish, but my family is not very religious. I tried asking my mom about everything that was going on and how it related to our faith. At the time, I didn't feel like she had suggestions that would help me. I then started to do some light research on what I could do. Please keep in mind that this all took place in the 1990s, which was before any of the paranormal shows began to air or had become popular. Most of the information that I found was based on Christian beliefs, and I felt that is was of no help at the time.

One day, I was hanging out with my good friend and his girlfriend. We were at her house, and I noticed some things that I thought were strange things in her bedroom like tarot cards, crystals, and other artifacts. When I asked her about them, I learned that she was Wiccan. We were talking about it for a while, and I ended up telling her about my experiences. She gave me some things to try. I don't remember everything she said, but I remember her suggesting putting salt around my bed and the couch on which I slept. She also told me that when I go into my home or go into my bedroom and I feel like there is something following me, if tell the spirit that this is my home and they are not welcome then that should keep it from entering. I tried both of those suggestions. They did help for a short time, but things were still happening.

There was a girl I dated for a short time. She was a normal girl, lived a normal suburban life, and was a happy person. She came over to my house one day and was sitting in a chair in my bedroom when she started talking about suicide. She then started to try and get sharp objects and started threatening to kill herself right there in my bedroom! Not knowing how to handle the situation, I ran and got my sister. My sister is no stranger to depression, and I knew if anyone could help, she could. My sister's advice was to call her parents and have them come get her. So, I did just that, and her parents took her to a nearby hospital. I spoke to her a couple of times after that. Once, she had told me that her parents blamed me for her actions and she was no longer allowed to talk to me. I decided to never speak to her again. Knowing what I know now, I can't help but wonder if she was being influenced by what was in my home.

As time went on, I was still having nightmares. I was still feeling like something was standing over me while I slept. I also felt like I was constantly being followed. I was fed up and feeling angry about this "thing" that was following me. So, I started yelling at it and cursing at it. For instance, when I entered my home I would say, "Stay the 'f' out! This is my home, not yours."

I would also tell it to leave me alone and stay out of my space as I would enter my bedroom. I was yelling and swearing at it more and more as time went on. My mom would tell me not to yell at the presence and it would leave me alone. Looking back, I wish that I had listened to her.

One night, I was sleeping on the couch in our living room. I had just put some fresh salt around the couch. That night I had what is the most terrifying experience that I have ever encountered. While I was laying down and sleeping, I felt like something was trying to enter my body. I was sleeping and realized I had to fight this feeling. I thought of the time my sister and her friend were using the Ouija Board and it said I was a challenge. I realized this is what it wanted. It wanted me, my soul...my body.

I knew I was sleeping. I told myself that I had to wake up. I then forced myself to wake up, but it was still attacking me. I quickly realized that I was still sleeping. At this time, I feel like I was fighting for my body and my soul. I forced myself to wake up three or four times in my dream. I suddenly woke up screaming and out of breath. I wondered, "Did I win?"

After that things seemed to settle down. I was still being watched, my favorite things would still disappear at times, but it was nowhere near as intense. I then went back to my Wiccan friend. She said that I just needed to ignore it and that it was probably feeding on my anger and fear. So, I tried to do that very thing.

It was now my senior year in high school. I met a girl and we became pretty serious. We both shared our paranormal experiences with one another. One particular time, we were in her bedroom, and she was telling me about her experiences in her home. In her bedroom she had a huge clock that was also a mirror. I don't know why, but I turned and looked at the clock. When I did, I had noticed that the hands were moving round and round. The arms of the clock moved very quickly; it was definitely weird. I got up to take to batteries out of the clock except there were no batteries in the clock! I decided to just take the clock down and turned it around so it was facing the wall.

Another time we were at my condo. It was a beautiful night, and we had decided to go for a night time walk in the park across the street. As we were walking, we stopped at a picnic table that was by the playground. We were both just sitting and talking. Out of the corner of my eye. I saw a large hooded man squatting with both feet on a railing of the playground equipment. Not believing what I had just seen, I did a double take and looked again. There was nothing or nobody there. I didn't feel threatened, so I shrugged it off as being my imagination.

As we were walking back to my place, there was a large hooded man sitting on the sit-up bench. His head was down, and we could not see his face. Again, I did not feel threatened, so I said, "Hi, how's it going?"

The man responded with just a grunt. We both stopped walking and looked at each other, then turned to look to back where the man was sitting there, but he was gone. This was a large wide-open park. There is no way a man that large could disappear so quickly. We then rushed back to my place.

We ended up getting an apartment together in Aurora, Ohio. Several months later, we then had a pretty nasty break up, and I moved to Phoenix, Arizona, with one of my best friends.

I lived in Phoenix from the year 2000 to 2003. The entire time I lived in Arizona I did not experience anything frightening or unexplained. I don't even remember having even one of the nightmares.

When I moved back to Ohio, I moved back in with my mom except this time I was using my sisters' old bedroom. Sure enough, right away, the nightmares started again. After a couple of nights, not thinking of the previous times that my money had disappeared, I put a $100 dollar bill that I wanted to save in my bedside table drawer, and when I woke up it was gone. To this day, I joke with my mom about there being a pile of money and band shirts inside the walls of the condo.

On a summer night, a friend and I decided that we wanted to go out and do some night fishing. I suggested we just go across the street of my place in the Chagrin River. My friend met me at my place, and we grabbed our fishing rods and tackle boxes. We crossed the street and headed over to the river. As we got close to the river bank, there was a row of tall bushes and tall grass. Just as we approached the bushes, they all shook violently. It was a calm summer night and there was no wind at all. Both of us with our eyes open wide, said in unison, "Nope!" and turned around and walked back to the condo.

I had just moved my tv and couch into my bedroom from the storage unit, so we decided to watch a couple movies instead of fishing that night. A couple years later my friend told me that after I had fallen asleep watching one of the movies that night he had to use the bathroom. The bathroom in my bedroom was out of service so my buddy went to use the bathroom in the hallway that was across from my old bedroom. When he went to open the door to the bathroom, he noticed that the light was on and the door was locked. Thinking that someone was in the bathroom he sat on my couch where he could see when they were done and left the bathroom. He said that a half hour later no one came out and the light stayed on. A while later he noticed that the light was turned off. He thought it was odd because no one ever came out of the bathroom, but he got up and tried to open the door and it was unlocked. He stated that is why he never came back over to that place.

At that time, I would still enter my room I would and say out loud, "This is my space and you are not welcome here! Stay out!" Only then would I close my door. In this bedroom, it was different. After I would do that I would feel very uneasy. It was like I was upsetting the spirit. So, I stopped demanding it to stay out and I also stopped closing the bedroom door all of the way. Then one night, I was in bed trying to go to sleep. I was laying in my bed with my eyes open when I suddenly saw a tall shadow figure walk into my room. The dark shadow figure walked across my room, turned and looked at me, then took a couple more steps and disappeared into the walk-in closet.

I am not exactly sure how tall it was. It was definitely taller than the doorway, and it had long arms and was darker than the room was with all of the lights turned off. It also had no face that I could see. I was petrified. I rolled over so that I was facing the wall. I was a 23 or 24 year old man, and I hid under my blankets like a child until the sun came out the next morning. That was the one and only time that I ever saw anything like that again.

When I was 25 years old, I met my wife, and by this time I had gotten my own apartment. When we got married, she moved in with me. When I was 30 we had our first daughter. Soon after our daughter was born and my wife was pregnant with our son, we bought our first home together. It was a trailer in Streetsboro, Ohio. As crazy or even as stupid as it sounds, we bought the trailer from the same friend that had been using the Ouija Board with my sister. She sold it to us dirt cheap and we needed more space, so it was the right choice for us at that time.

One night, when my daughter was four years old, I noticed she was sitting up in her bed and talking as if someone was in the room with her. As I listened closer, I heard her say, "But, no, I don't want to."

By this time, the ghost hunting shows had been playing on tv and were starting to get popular, so I got the idea to get a digital recorder app for my phone. I hit the record button and asked, "Is someone talking to my daughter?"

I played it back and heard a response that was clear as day, "Yes."

I thought to myself, no way am I going to let my daughter be terrorized like I had been. My mom had a friend in town whom she had just recently met and was a Native American shaman. I told him what had happened with my daughter. He said that my mom had mentioned something to him about things that were happening at her new place as well. After coming to both of our houses, he called me and said, "Shawn we have to talk."

He said that in his meditation he saw an attachment to my entire family from our old home. He then asked me what happened there. I told him about the old condo and my sister and her friend using the Ouija Board and that I bought the trailer from the same friend that used the Ouija board with my sister. So, the shaman did a cleansing on me, my home and my mom's home. He wanted to take a Native American spirit wheel that was hanging up on a wall that my wife had bought me on a trip that we took to Arizona. He said that the spirit can use it to attach itself to it, so I let him take it. He said that he buried it and that I can't know where it is.

A month later we ended up selling the trailer for $2000 and shortly after that moved into our "forever home".

I have not felt that presence or any other presence like it since then.

I have since been baptized Catholic and am now stronger spiritually than ever before. I now investigate the paranormal and try to help people that experience fear like did when I was younger.

Later, my sister did admit to not only using the Ouija Board inside of the condo, both in her bedroom and even in my bedroom when I was not home. She also still says that they were just playing around and nothing ever came of them using the Ouija Board.

Shawn Gilmore is an empath and a paranormal investigator. His profound experiences growing up as a child and into his young adult ages are what lead him to researching and investigating the paranormal. He lived his life being terrified of his home for many years. Shawn feels that if he understood the experiences differently, things could have been a lot better for himself and his family during his adolescent years. Now Shawn investigates the paranormal in hopes to help other people understand that the paranormal is actually just normal.

Shawn was born in San Diego, California, but as a child he and his family moved to northeast Ohio where he currently lives with his family of three beautiful children and his wife of over a decade. Most of his time is spent with his family; hiking, camping, playing sports, games, and anything else to enjoy being with his wife and children.

Calling Out Bob

John Ward

Let me begin by saying that for the first 20 years of my life I was a total skeptic and disbeliever in the paranormal. I had never experienced anything supernatural and had no reason to believe in ghosts, spirits, or anything paranormal in nature. I dismissed every story that anyone had ever told me, and I always said that I'd have to experience something for myself in order to believe in anything.

In May of 2011, I moved into an apartment in Akron, Ohio, with a buddy of mine. His name is Shaun. Before I get into everything, let me give you a description of the two-story apartment itself. As soon as you walked in the door, the living room was to your left and there was an open area that could be used as a dining room, but we left empty. To the left of that was our kitchen, and to the right was the staircase that led up to my roommate's bedroom. There was also a walkway by the staircase that led to my bedroom. Shaun's room was right on top of mine.

Now that you have somewhat of a visual of my apartment, let me begin by telling you the back story. My roommate and I worked together at a factory in Wadsworth, Ohio, on the same second shift and would always talk at work. One day out of the blue, Shaun told me, "I think Bob followed me again."

I shot him a puzzled look and asked him who Bob was, and he proceeded to tell me that it was a spirit that has followed him everywhere he has lived his entire life.

I laughed at him and figured he was just trying to scare me. I mean seriously, a spirit named Bob? (I guess that was what he had named the spirit as a kid.)

So, I'm standing there giving him a hard time about it and poking fun at him about it, and he simply says, "Bob doesn't like it when people disrespect him and don't believe."

The smirk on his face is a memory that will always be engrained in my head.

I dismissed it and said, "Yeah, yeah, whatever. If Bob is real then he can come meet me anytime."

Little did I know at the time what I had coming my way. My life would never be the same.

I continued giving Shaun a hard time about the Bob situation for several days and nothing happened. I kept making fun of him and kept on calling out Bob, both at home and at work. I now regret doing so because things went from occurrences happening that could be explained to things that, to this day, give me chills and I cannot explain.

It all started around July 2011, with small events happening like things being moved from their normal spots, to lights being on when we got home from work that weren't on when we left. (We worked second shift at the time.)

These things puzzled me, but it never scared or startled me. Actually, after a while, I forgot about the whole Bob thing. until one day we were at the bar down the road from our apartment with Shaun's previous roommate and, somehow, we got on the topic of Bob. His old roommate started telling me stories of strange, unexplainable occurrences that happened to him when he lived with Shaun. Again, I dismissed things and laughed it off. Nothing happened that night either.

A couple nights later, my girlfriend at the time (now my wife), Hilary, and I were in the apartment alone watching *Paranormal Activity*, ironically enough, and at the end of the movie we heard footsteps upstairs in Shaun's bedroom. She shot me a half-scared, half-grinning, "Are you kidding me?" kind of look.

I had never told Hilary about Bob because I didn't believe in him at the time, and I told her it was probably just the neighbors. We laughed it off and told ourselves it was just our minds playing a trick on us. The noises stopped, and we joked and laughed it off then went to go to bed. That same night, while still alone in the apartment, we were lying there in the dark about to go to sleep, trying to wind down, when all of a sudden a loud BANG hit my door *really* loud. It sounded like someone threw a hard punch into my door.

Hilary looked at me and asked, "What was that?"

She totally freaked out. I'm not going to lie, this startled me pretty bad, as well. I told her it was just the movie getting in our heads. However, just to try to rationalize things, I opened the bedroom door.

Nobody was home, the lights were off, nothing was around my bedroom door. I couldn't explain this, but I told her just to ignore it and go to sleep. I'm not going to lie, I did not sleep well that night. I had a weird feeling that someone or something was watching me. Nothing else happened that night.

I told Shaun that next day what had happened and he laughed at me and said, "Bob don't like you, man, I told you not to call him out." His response left me scrambling.

I told him I thought Bob was just trying to scare me and what not, and Shaun shook his head and said, "Nope, and I told you not to call him out. He doesn't like that."

His response angered me, and I just walked away, irritated. I actually went home that night and apologized to Bob. I was starting to believe. Surprisingly, nothing happened for a while after that.

The next time something happened was that December. I had forgotten about the whole thing. One night, I was in the apartment, alone, smoking a cigarette in the living room. Shaun was at the bar and Hilary was back home on break from college. I finished my cigarette and went to go to my bedroom to grab a movie. As I reached the underpass walkway under Shaun's bedroom, I heard a loud BANG up in his bedroom. It sounded like a dresser had been slammed against the wall, that's how loud it was. I froze dead in my tracks. I heard footsteps upstairs. Then everything went quiet. I called Shaun and told him what happened, and I told him I wasn't going up there. I had never felt that kind of fear before.

At first, Shaun said, "Okay, I'll check it out when I get home," but as soon as he said that, he told me to at least go check and make sure his pet lizard was okay.

I reluctantly agreed to go and check on his pet lizard, and I hung up the phone. I walk up the stairs, and what I saw shocked me. *Nothing* can explain what happened.

I got up there, and the first thing I noticed was a picture that he had hung up on the wall had somehow flown off the wall and landed at least ten feet to the right, the glass on it shattered all around. I then went to the opposite corner of his room where his lizard tank was, and this shocked me even more. Somehow the heat lamp that rested flat on top of his lizard cage had flown off the top of the cage and through a small opening between the legs and cross bar of his dresser, which was a couple feet to the right of the tank. It lay on the ground, and its bulb was shattered. This was in the middle of winter, *in Ohio*. We didn't have windows open, there was no air drafts. I cannot think of an explanation for this.

I called Shaun back and told him what got broken there. He got mad and yelled at me for angering Bob. I defended myself, said that I apologized and everything went back to normal for a while, and Shaun said that it didn't matter because Bob didn't like me.

I got off the phone and left the apartment freaked out. The absolute level of fear I felt from that night still remains unexplainable, and I cannot put a proper word on it to state what I truly felt that night. I called Hilary and finally filled her in about Bob as I walked out. She was freaked out by what I was telling her since she was a firm believer in the paranormal.

Nothing happened after this for a while aside from little things, which we always took as Bob just being mischievous.

The next major occurrence happened one day in March. I was at work, sweating in the hot factory, when I suddenly felt my back burning. I didn't think much of it until after work when I got out of the shower and Hilary asked, "Oh my god, what did you do to your back?"

I shot her a puzzled look, and I told her, "Nothing," and asked why. Hilary then took a picture of my back with her phone and showed me. I had a pair of three claw marks stretching down each side of my mid to lower back. This scared me because we didn't have pets that could have done that, and Hilary and I hadn't done anything the night before that would have caused it. We were both pretty scared, but I played it off like it didn't frighten me. At the time, I didn't know the severity of what those marks meant.

Things went quiet again for a while, and nothing happened for about a month. We were all sitting around in the living room with friends talking about Bob because he'd been pulling his little pranks the previous few nights. Shaun and everyone else headed out to the bar that night, and Hilary and I stayed in to relax.

We were getting ready to go to sleep when an alarm suddenly started going off upstairs in Shaun's room. I ran upstairs, cursing at Bob and telling him to knock it off! I thought it was the smoke alarm when I got up there, but it wasn't. It was a music player Shaun hooked his phone up to all the time. I unplugged speaker and the alarm stopped.

I called Shaun and told him what happened so he wouldn't think I was touching his stuff, and he told me, "Dude, that thing doesn't have an alarm on it."

Chills went up my spine, but that was the very last occurrence I had with Bob. We moved out a month later, and Hilary and I got our own place.

The events that I went through were both terrifying and unexplainable. Those unexplainable paranormal occurrences are what made me decide to become a paranormal investigator and to try to find answers to these experiences and what happens after death.

Needless to say, having unexplainable paranormal occurrences changed my life forever and turned me from a skeptic...into a firm believer!

John Ward co-founder of his paranormal team, Ohio Paranormal Syndicate (OPS), works independently with other teams on investigations, and also works on some side projects to further provide proof of the paranormal. He loves a challenge and loves trying to communicate and provide proof of life after death, even when science dictates and says it isn't possible. John is a lifelong resident in Northeast Ohio, and is married to his wife whom is also a paranormal investigator alongside him.

The Renwick Mansion

Katie Hopkins

We (the Unknown Darkness Team) were on the lookout for new locations to investigate in 2018. When I say new, I mean new to us, not new to paranormal investigations. When we stumbled upon the Renwick Mansion we were really excited that one. We had never investigated it before, the owners are extremely nice (plus no one had investigated under them as the owners before), and they were open to not only a private investigation, but they also allowed us to hold an event there that is open to guests!

The mansion was built in 1877 by William Renwick who took over a lumber and sawmill business founded by his father, James, an immigrant from England. The building is Davenport, Iowa's, finest example of Italian Revival Villa architecture, featuring a large fourth-story tower that overlooks Davenport and the Mississippi River, amazing wooden trim, 12-14 foot doors, eight bedrooms, eight fireplaces, a three story staircase, a limestone exterior, and it sits on four acres in the heart of Davenport. In 1907, the mansion became part of St. Katharine's School, and in 1973 was sold and became part of a nursing home complex. Although it was listed on the National Register of historic places in 1983, the home fell into disrepair. The ailing complex was purchased by a historic property developer in 1997, who renovated the St. Katherine's location and the Renwick House. In 2007, the Renwick was updated with geothermal and opened to the public as a wedding reception venue and bed and breakfast. After closing in

2016, the Renwick House was opened once again in 2017 as a premier location for weddings, receptions, reunions, parties, and meetings.

The keyword in that history is limestone. They say that limestone has the ability to absorb energy and also provide energy for spirits. Also, the mansion sits on top of a hill that overlooks the Mississippi River. Water is another energy source for spirits. Needless to say, this was a hotspot for paranormal activity with the elements and also the history behind the structure and land.

On July 25, 1901, a fire erupted throughout the east side of town causing over a million dollars of damage. This fire did not consume any lives, but a lot of hope was lost. The fire stopped just as it got to the hill that the mansion sits upon. This would become "sacred ground" and those in the town would come there to pray on the land, another event that aids the activity in the home.

My journey at the Renwick Mansion began before we even got there. One day, I was trying to remote view the Renwick Mansion to see if I could "see" any spirits there. I wasn't having much luck and reached out to psychic medium Vanessa Hogle for advice. She told me that not every location is going to "come to me" as easily as others. She said I may never get a remote vision from there, and that's okay. I tend to be able to visualize better with locations that have had trauma. There are many reasons as to why this is. It could be the type of spirits there are more open to "showing" themselves, or it could be that I am more open to those types of spirits and wanting to hear their stories. The possibilities are endless as to why I can see what I see.

Just because I couldn't see any spirits there the one day I had tried doesn't mean I was going to give up. I tried again one day, while looking at a picture of the mansion. Suddenly, I got a sharp pain in my head. It was on the left temple; I was seeing head trauma.

I quickly emailed the owner to ask her if there had ever been anyone who fell down the stairs, or even worse, was shot in the head. She said she didn't know of any incidents where this happened, but she also said she doesn't have much detailed history of the home. I wanted to find out more as to why I was seeing someone with head trauma. Whether it was someone from the senior condominiums next door or just from somewhere in the vicinity. Why was I seeing this?

The day of the investigation arrived, and we were ready to head to Davenport for the investigation. We picked up our teammates Shannon and Sarah and got on the road. We arrived at the mansion early so we could get some daytime shots of it for the promotional videos we like to make. There were some people there setting up for a baby shower the next day, and I asked them if they had every witnessed anything there. One said they saw a door slam shut before in room seven.

Other than that, there wasn't much from them. This is different from our usual investigations as we are used to multiple stories and experiences. This just gave us a clean slate to experience our own events without "persuasion" from other experiences.

We got our DVR cameras setup and then it was time for dinner, so we locked up the mansion and left to go find a restaurant. We ended up at a Mexican Grill that was really good. Usually we don't usually eat Mexican food before investigations due to the "stomach demons," but we didn't really have another option as all other restaurants had a long wait, and we needed to get back and investigate.

We got back after dinner and, naturally, Shannon had setup a recorder while we'd been gone. He didn't listen back to the recorder until on our way home, but we caught quite the voice while we were gone. There was the voice of a young woman on the recorder, not too far from it either. She talks for about 10 seconds, stops, and then talks again. Shannon describes it as an EVP that's "out of this world." This was not the only EVP we caught that evening.

As the investigation progressed, we kept getting the feeling of being watched. We started off in the parlor area on the main floor where we caught the EVP's from earlier, but also another one. This time it was a man's voice. It was a very deep voice and we caught it while doing an EVP blast in the parlor on the left. It is closest to the kitchen, so this makes me think it was, at one point, a formal dining room. It is not clear what the voice is saying, but it is definitely there trying to communicate.

We decided to split up and go to the basement. With Sarah, Hannah (teammate and my sister-in-law), and I were the ones that headed downstairs. We started off with the ghost box, and we were getting some voices coming through, but they came through so fast it was hard to make them out. Then my "seeing" started. Suddenly, I started to picture a man walking around in the basement. He didn't know we were there, however. It was almost like he could sense our energy just like I sensed his, but he couldn't see us. He followed us around the basement. I let him follow us for a little bit before I acknowledged him and told Sarah and Hannah about him.

He wasn't very tall, maybe 5'7", and he was crooked. He was hunched over but to the side, like his spine was crooked. He was also limping, and he had long greasy hair that hung in front of his face. He didn't really have much of an expression, but I could tell he was not very comfortable. It makes me wonder if he was from the St. Katherine Nursing Home time period. Maybe he had scoliosis or something? I am not sure. He would take a deep breath and let it out, and just keep walking. He was harmless, and he could definitely have been residual. Why he was in the basement? I have no clue.

We took a break and went upstairs. We collected our thoughts and had a few snacks. We then went upstairs to room number seven. This is where they said a door had slammed shut, and also, they'd felt a lot of energy in that room. Sarah, Hannah, Joy (my mother-in-law), and I were in that room together. It was pretty quiet. We did get a few ghost box hits, but nothing too crazy. We had the K2 setup but we did not get anything on that.

The only area to provide K2 hits was in the basement, which is the next portion of the chapter. We were wondering if we would get any more activity and were thinking of calling it a night. Then, Josh and I decided to go down to the basement. Josh and I used to investigate as just the two of us way back in our early stages of investigating, so we thought, let's do it like the "old days." We used to get activity like crazy when it was just us two. We're not sure if we are just magnets for the paranormal or if we just chose all the right nights!

During this time, we were also doing a live feed on Facebook, and I had the flash on my camera so people could see what was going on. We went back to where the old coal chute was in the basement and set up the K2. It would not stop. So, we figured there was just a high amount of electricity that was setting it off. When

Josh went to go grab it, it stopped. At this time, the owners of the mansion also came down to the basement. We informed them what the K2 was used for and told them what was happening. We were also talking about the other experiences we'd had throughout the evening. They had to leave to a friend's birthday party, so they said goodbye and Josh and I stayed in the basement. However, we moved over to a different room where the electric panels are located. We did not use the K2 in that room since the electric panels radiate a high electromagnetic field that would contaminate the K2.

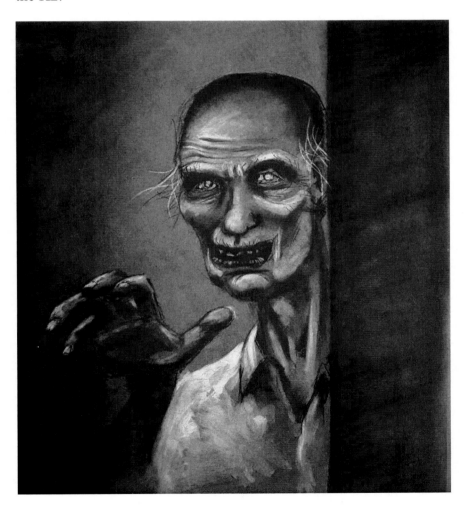

We stood there with the flash still on my camera. Josh wanted to see what it would be like shutting the light off, but he wanted to stand back to back as he felt anything could surprise us at any moment. He was facing towards the electric panels and I was facing the room that was next to us which had a fire pit for the eight fireplaces in the home. I shut off the flash and it wasn't even a minute later that the energy shifted.

The hair on my arms stood straight up, and I told Josh what I was seeing. I was sensing a very familiar energy that I had encountered before at the Buchanan County Home. However, I wasn't sure if this was the same guy or not. His energy was the same, but I could only see his shadow. I couldn't see his features like I had at the Buchanan. This energy almost had me in tears as well, and I am not one to just break out into tears. It had also been a while since a spirit energy had done that to me. Josh also told me that when the lights went out, he felt a hand grab his shoulder which also made his shoulder hot. I told Josh what I had "seen," showed him my arm hair, and he asked if we should go upstairs. I told him yes, we probably should. This was the only encounter that night which had that type of energy. Everything else was light and playful.

That was the last encounter I had that evening. I wasn't sure if I could take much more as that drained my energy pretty well. We packed up our equipment and headed home for the night.

Katie Hopkins is a paranormal investigator with Unknown Darkness. She has appeared on *Ghost Adventures* at Edinburgh Manor, *Paranormal Encounters: Edinburgh Manor*, *My Ghost Story*, has been featured on the local news in Cedar Rapids, IA, and was recently interviewed for *The Paranormal Diaries*. Her book *Seeing Spirits: Opening the Emapthic Door* was published by Haunted Road Media in 2018.

My First Time

Tammy Heitzmann

After years of researching the paranormal, including listening to and learning from some of whom I consider to be the best in the field, I signed up for my first official "ghost hunt." In preparation, I collected a few basic "tools of the trade," including a digital voice recorder, a spirit box, and video camera with night vision. First and foremost, however, I knew that my own senses would be the most reliable tool. I was right!

On September 15, 2017, two friends and I made our way to the USS Cobia (SS-245), a US Navy WWII submarine that boasted six war patrols during her deployment. Having housed soldiers and prisoners of war, alike, she has a rich history, and I was excited to investigate her. Rumor had it that, over the years, there has been a good amount of paranormal activity on the submarine, but this was the very first official ghost hunt conducted on her, and I felt honored to be a part of it.

There was one group ahead of us, and while we (impatiently) waited, we investigated the adjoined Maritime Museum. There ended up being too much contamination, however, in our evidence, so we weren't able to definitively uncover any activity.

The USS Cobia, however, was a different story. Upon entering the Cobia, we were met by those who'd just gone through, and every group, according to what they said, had experienced something. From being touched to voice evidence, we heard some great stories. It wasn't until my own experience that I knew for

151

certain that the USS Cobia definitely has at least one permanent guest. Let me tell you, he wants to be heard, and I would venture to say, I believe he enjoys the attention, or the company, or the chance to communicate!

We decided to do an EVP session in the rec area of the sub. We'd heard that this area seemed to contain much of the activity, along with the stern. I sat, straddled, on a bench, which was connected to a table. It was, basically, a small, metal picnic table. I had my EVP recorder in my left hand, my elbow resting on the table, and my hand slightly in front of my face, mic facing away from me. While greeting whoever might be hanging around, hoping and wondering if we'd be lucky enough to speak with "Ralph," the only soldier documented as being shot by the enemy, and later dying, on the Cobia, I got the most amazing chill on my arm. It wasn't like any other cold feeling or chill I'd ever felt. There was no breeze, and it was an instant "cold to the bone" feeling, isolated to my arm. I made sure I verbalized what I was feeling, and I'm glad I did.

Prompted by what I had just felt, we explained that we were all there to meet him or her. At that exact moment, I heard, in my own left ear, what sounded like a loud whisper. There was no mistaking it. In addition, at the exact same time, I felt a rush of energy, much like what you might feel being in front of very loud speakers, minus the breeze. I asked my friend if she heard what I'd heard, and she responded that she did not. I didn't want to interrupt the audio, or fail to capture any audio evidence, so I kept recording. I didn't actually know what was said, or if I'd even captured it on audio, until I got home and played it back. Low and behold, I captured my first, what I can say was legitimate, EVP!

After that experience, we continued our session, and after a little time, we made our way down the sub. On our way back through, heading toward where we originally entered the sub, I made it a point to take as many pictures as I could (I couldn't figure out how to work the camera correctly, at first, but we won't talk about that!). I took a lot of pictures in each section of the sub. It turned out that our sociable spirit, who may or may not be "Ralph," or whoever this person is, is also not camera shy. I am happy to say, I got a picture of him peeking through an entryway in one of my photos!

Much like any evidence, two people can interpret the same EVP, or other proof, differently. I had several people listen to the EVP I captured, without knowing the background about where I got it, one of them being our beloved psychic medium, Vanessa Hogle. While I heard, "hey there," she heard and felt, "please don't eat me."

Although what I heard coincides with the ongoing conversation the moment I captured the EVP, Vanessa's take on it leads to other interesting possibilities. In my research of the Cobia, I found that they picked up at least one Japanese prisoner of war, who, according to official, publicly released documentation, was released to proper authorities at the submarine's next stop. Here's the thing. Also, in my research, I found that cannibalism was common on Japanese submarines and ships, specifically during WWII. Could our spirit be a POW who was killed on board, or even worse, the victim of cannibalism? Was it actually 19-year old Ralph, or someone else saying, "hey there," like I thought I heard? Perhaps I will never know for certain.

I do know, for certain, that I was ecstatic about what I captured on my very first "ghost hunt." Verbalization of what I physically felt and heard, along with the EVP evidence I was able to record, substantiates what I know. There is a spirit on the USS Cobia who is eager to communicate!

A Strange Encounter

Diane Hilbert

Back in the early 1970s in Rhode Island, rumors flew about a house a druid priest had built at the end of a dead-end street in Narragansett. It is believed that his surname was Hazard and he had fled Salem, Massachusetts, around the time of the witch hunts. *Bad things happened here*

One of the rumors said that three students from the University of Rhode Island had broken into the old abandoned house and spent the night there on a dare. In the morning, the veins on their wrists each had the sign of the Devil. Within the next three years, each of these young men died a very violent death.

One fall afternoon in 1972, my fiancé and I, along with another couple, decided to take a long ride and check out this place out. This was long before the invention of the GPS, so we relied on a road map, and yes, we eventually found it. The house looked like it was made of stone, and to us, it seemed massive. It happened to be the last house on the left, although at that time, there were very few houses on the road, and they were widely spaced apart from one another. The road just ended after the house with cliffs and the Atlantic Ocean right there in front of you. Directly across the road from the house was a wooded area.

We got out of our car and began to explore around a bit. The house appeared to be abandoned with sheets over furniture and huge cob webs as far as you could see inside the ground floor windows. The property was very unkempt, but I am sure it was once beautiful. We noticed the roof of the house formed a peak, and there was a window under it.

My fiancé, Ed, a budding young photographer who always had his 35mm Nikon around his neck, decided to look at things through the zoom lens for a better view. To our astonishment, there was what looked like satanic symbols or something on those window panes on that upper window. He began to take lots of pictures.

After we finished poking around the property, we headed back to the car and our friend Dave noticed there was a clearing in the wooded area across from the house. I wanted to check that out, too, since we were there. Why not, right? Stepping maybe ten feet into the clearing we noticed some kind of stone altar. There were eight columns evenly spaced around the altar that appeared to be made of stone with a hollowed-out bowl shape on top of each one. Turning to look back at the house, we realized that this altar was in direct alignment with that upper window.

Our minds began to speculate that because it was said this man was a druid, maybe he conducted sacrifices from his window as he looked down into those woods. Why else would there be such an altar in the woods? As we were discussing the possibilities, we heard a strange voice, not one of our own say, "Get out!"

We turned and there was a man in 1600s clothing with the biggest German shepherd-type dog bearing the biggest teeth I'd ever seen. "Get out of here!" he repeated.

As he turned to leave the clearing, we all followed. There was only ten feet to the road, we were on his heels, but he just vanished with nowhere he could have gone.

Spooked beyond our wits, we got in the car and just drove and drove, finally making it home. Still shaking, we decided to develop the film to see what we'd captured. Ed had his own dark room at the time and always did his own developing. When we finished processing the pictures, all we had was that upper window with no symbols on the panes, yet we all saw them with the zoom lens. We did have a few pictures of the clearing in the woods with the stone altar and pillars, but they were barely visible on the film.

We have never returned to Hazzard Blvd., nor do any of us want to.

First Encounter With

A Spirit

Betty Langy

1st Visitation

I was about five and sleeping late. What child doesn't love ignoring chores and snoozing late? I glanced up because something felt different or strange from normal sleep. At the foot of the bed was an indescribable thing for a five-year old. So, here was my first encounter; see through, tall, sparkly, SCARY. I did what any normal child would do. I pulled the covers over my head and whispered, "Go away." It did.

2nd Visitation, next morning

That morning was gloomy. Cold outside met cold inside. One small stove warmed our home that spring. This second visitation started the same as the morning before. I was attempting to sleep in to keep warm, but something cold kept touching my feet. I pulled down the covers and saw IT again. This time, I saw eyes that stared right into me. "Ask me!" I heard its voice demand. I felt scared to death, literally, pulled the covers over my head and wet the bed. The covers stayed there until Mother came to wake me up.

3rd and Last Visitation, third morning

Once again, I was sleeping. In my home, I was the seventh child of a seventh child, my mother. Older sisters, older brothers, and seven nieces and nephews made up my life now. My bed was shared by others. To get to sleep past 6:00 AM was a miracle. Television was new, so it was seldom on. On the third morning, I woke up feeling different, not scared, but curious. Before me stood the vision, and angrily I asked, "What do you want?" without words because my bed was shared.

The vision said, "I have come to protect you, Will you accept me?"

"Why?" I asked.

"Because you will need me."

Remember now, I am a five-year old who feared this vision.

"Who are you?" I asked, very curious.

"I am Jesus," it said.

Understand, no words were spoken just understood. I nodded because I wanted IT to leave. IT left.

That morning, I asked my mother who was Jesus? I'd had no formal training in my home about ordained religion. No one spoke to me about Jesus. My mother came to understand that I needed to learn about IT.

Two years later, my oldest brother died. He was my favorite brother, 12 years my senior. Six months later, my mother fought for her life from cancer. I was seven. I'd gone to Sunday school for two years by then. During my mother's hospital stays, my brother closest to me started a seven-year abuse toward me.

During those painful times, the IT named Jesus came and held me close, took me away from the pain and kept me sane. For me, after a lifetime of searching for answers about religion and spirituality, being so different from normal peers, I came to understand my first encounter with Spirit saved my life. I've been down many avenues seeking answers and have found many wonderful teachers, lived through many encounters with SPIRIT in many forms, and am still learning as I live the last quarter of my life. From Christian to Wiccan to Pagan, I have been blessed to enjoy not being normal since my first encounter with SPIRIT.

Paranormal Encounter

Vignettes

(Multiple Contributors)

<u>LinzWhite</u>:

I was at work and lying in a chair with the foot stool laid out to where it can make a bed. I put the coffee table up against it to keep it from sliding out from under me, and that's where I sit or lay. It is right in front of the staff room which is the extra bedroom we use for staff. It has a closet.

So, I had fallen asleep and in a weird dream I found myself in the staff room closet doorway. I couldn't move at all. I'm was just stuck there, standing there.

It took all I had to try to move only a few inches. In all my other dreams, I am like an observer, looking down at myself and at whatever is going on. But this dream was different.

When I finally get myself to move some (it was very little), I found myself back in the chair on which I had fallen asleep. At this point in the dream, I still couldn't move. I was facing the doorway to the staff room and I was lying in the chair when someone or something crawled in behind me. It wrapped itself around me and started touching my head and face. It was petting me in a very weird way. I couldn't move or speak.

Finally, I thought the word "STOP" really loud inside my head, and whatever or whoever it was slowly moved off of me and I sat up, awake, thinking, "What just happened?"

Now, I think of myself as a bit of an empath and intuitive, and I have seen things out of the corner of my eye from time to time. However, I have never experienced anything like that dream I had that night at work.

Donna Marie:

I was a ghost hunter for 5 years with RTS Paranormal, and our base was on the *USS Salem* (CA-139). This ship is at bay in Quincy, Massachusetts. Now, I did see shadow people on this ship. This ship went to Greece after a bad earthquake and was filled all the injured. One time, when I was down in the brig someone was playing with my hair. I didn't freak. After all, I wanted an experience. I did get one, but I had no idea what else I was in for that night. I went outside to have a cigarette, and when I looked up there was a senior officer saluting me. I will never forget this. I was so excited to prove to myself ghosts and spirits do exist.

"beat3airspace":

In 1959, when I was about five years old, my family and I moved to a big, new, farmhouse with a really cool attic. I was the baby of seven children and slept in my parents' room on an antique 3/4 bed, which was built by my great grandfather's great grandfather. My mother, great aunt, grandmother, and other women of the family, were believers in Spiritualism. One of them read tea leaves and coffee grounds. My aunt once rubbed a sliced potato on my brother's elbow, seasoned the potato with spices, and buried it during a waxing moon phase to get rid of warts on his elbow. They disappeared in a week. These occurrences were common in my house and I thought of them as normal. My family went to church. My father was a deacon and a board member. My sisters and my mother sang in the choir. We had a thriving farm, but to this day, I still hate chickens. Everyone in the community could see that we were a happy family, although a little different. There were always people coming over for dinner or just to visit. My father and brothers were always helping other families, friends, and even strangers.

One early autumn night, I awoke to the sensation of my covers being pulled off of me. At first, I was frightened, and it seemed like a lot of time had passed before I was able to open my eyes. When I looked, I saw an older lady dressed in pioneer period clothing, and she was smiling at me. I screamed very loudly for my mother, which woke up everyone else in the house. My brothers got out their trusty Brownie cameras and decided to sleep on the floor and wait for this "intruder" to visit again. They did this for four nights straight until my father told them to go back to their own beds. On the fifth night, however, she showed up again, and this time I followed her into our huge country kitchen. I watched as she pointed to our giant cast iron stove and its deep well. I have fond memories of my mother cooking stew, chili, mustard greens and all kinds of lip-smacking goodies in that deep well. I went to my father, shook him awake, and told him what I had just witnessed. He checked the well and saw that the default gas ignition was rusted. If my mother would have turned it on, the whole house would have exploded!! I was relieved and thankful for what the spirit of this unknown lady had shown me.

I was taught not to be too scared of spirits. My experience with that female apparition would end up being the first of many in the next fifty-eight years. I once saw an old brown-tinted photo in a family album. Imagine my surprise when I saw a picture of the spirit/intruder from my very first paranormal experience. She turned out to be my great-great-great-grandmother Shipp, the wife of the builder of my 3/4 antique bed.

Veronica Jaco:

I used to work in a psychiatric hospital for 12 years It had 12 rooms there for patients, plus one where I took naps. Several times when I was asleep, I felt a presence near me, and it was very evil. I could see it in my mind; he was very tall and dark black. When I felt him, I would tell him to go away and leave me alone, and I would ignore it. Well, one day I took a nap, and I felt him grab my feet and try to pull me down I don't know how many seconds or minutes it lasted, but it felt a long time until he let me go. That was my paranormal experience.

The
Ferry Plantation

Virginia Beach, Virginia

The Ferry Plantation House is a multi-generational historic mansion along the Lynnhaven River in Virginia Beach, Virginia. The oldest part of the building was once the Third Princess Anne Courthouse built in 1735, which saw use until 1751 when the stocks and pillory were taken to Newtown. It was added onto in 1830 as use for a home after an 1828 fire consumed the original manor house on the property. The manor house had been built in 1751 and bricks from it were used in the current home's construction. The final extension of the house was built in 1850.

The property dates back to 1642 when the second ferry service in Hampton Roads was started to carry passengers on the river to the county courthouse and local plantations. The Second Princess Anne Courthouse was also built on the property when it was much larger and is the location of the famous witch trial of Grace Sherwood who was finally pardoned in 2006.

Grace Sherwood:
The Witch of Pungo

Michelle Hamilton

When one thinks of witchcraft in the American colonies, the vision of the Salem, Massachusetts, Witch Trials of 1692 instantly spring to mind. Though the most famous, the Salem Witch Trials were not the only witch trials during the colonial period. The colony of Virginia also had throughout its early period, several, sporadic, cases of women being accused of witchcraft. Unlike, Massachusetts, the courts in Virginia were reluctant to hear accusations of witchcraft and demanded a much higher burden of proof. Though few records have survived, of the nineteen surviving court cases that dealt with witchcraft from the Seventeenth Century there was only one conviction for witchcraft, the other cases ended in the acquittal of the accused witch. Out of the few convictions in colonial Virginia no accused witch was executed and only one, Grace Sherwood, was given a trial by ducking.

Grace Sherwood was born 1660 likely in the community of Pungo, in Princess Anne County, the daughter of John and Susan White. John White was a successful carpenter and farmer. Today, Pungo is in the southern part of Virginia Beach, but in the Seventeenth Century the area was a sparsely populated area dotted with small farms clustered next to the Lynnhaven River. Life in

Seventeenth Century Virginia for the early English colonists was difficult and life the expectancy was short. With few doctors, the skills of a midwife who was knowledgeable of the use of herbs was essential.

In 1680, Grace White married James Sherwood in the Lynnhaven Parish Church. James Sherwood was a respected landowner. Though the Sherwood's were landowners, they were not wealthy. Grace gave birth to three sons, John, James, and Richard. To care for her family, Grace grew herbs and served the local community as a midwife, caring for her neighbors and their livestock. In 1701, James Sherwood died leaving his property to his wife. Following the death of her husband, Grace did not remarry.

Grace Sherwood was described by her contemporaries as attractive and possessing a sense of humor. She stood out for her unconventional behavior, instead of wearing a dress while working on her farm, she donned trousers. This along with her decision not to remarry and her knowledge of herbs made her stand out as unusual and aroused jealousy from the women in the community. Grace's behavior and her independence led to the witchcraft accusations that would plague her for the remainder of her life.

The first accusation of witchcraft against Grace Sherwood occurred in 1697, when a neighbor Richard Capps accused Grace of bewitching his bull. The sudden death of livestock on a farm in the Seventeenth Century was a serious issue. Though the case went to trial, the Princess Anne County court was unable to make a ruling. Angered at Richard Capps, John and Grace Sherwood sued for defamation. This was only the beginning of the witchcraft allegations, perhaps emboldened by Capps' accusation, others came forward with their accusations.

The next year in 1698, another neighbor John Gisburne accused Grace Sherwood of bewitching his pigs and cotton crop. Following this accusation, Elizabeth Barnes came forward and accused Grace of taking the form of a black cat that had entered her home. In the guise of the cat, Grace then jumped over Elizabeth Barnes' bed, whipped her, and then escaped the house through the keyhole. Despite the sensational allegations, the court still refused to make a ruling on the Gisburne and Barnes cases. The Sherwood's again sued for defamation but lost their cases against Gisburne and Barnes and the couple had to pay court-related expenses.

Grace Sherwood would not be brought to court again for several years. In 1705, Grace got into a dispute with her neighbor

Elizabeth Hill. The dispute turned violent, and Grace took Elizabeth Hill and her husband to court for assault and battery. Unlike in the other court cases that Grace had been involved with in the past, Grace won this court case and was awarded twenty shillings in damages on December 7, 1705. Instead of ending the dispute between the Hills and Grace Sherwood, the feud would only intensify. shortly after the December 1705 court case, Elizabeth Hill suffered a miscarriage. In Elizabeth's mind there was only one person responsible for the loss of her unborn child—Grace Sherwood.

On January 3, 1706, the Hills accused Grace Sherwood of witchcraft. Grace refused to appear in court for her third accusation of witchcraft and on February 7, 1706, the court ordered her to appear on a charge of witchcraft. This time the Princess Anne County Court did not dismiss the charges and in March 1706, empaneled two juries made up of women to investigate the accusations and to search for evidence. The first jury was ordered to search Grace's home for evidence of witchcraft. The second jury was instructed to search Grace's body for evidence of a witch's mark. A witch's mark, also known as a devil's mark, was any defect on the body of an accused with that was viewed as evidence that a person was touched by the devil and was a witch.

Naturally, the second jury found evidence of a witch's mark on Grace Sherwood's body. The jury declared that they had discovered two "marks not like theirs or like those of any other woman." Despite these findings, the colonial courts were reluctant to declare that Grace was a witch. The court case dragged on for months as Grace was shuttled between one court to another with no definitive ruling made. On May 2, 1706, Grace was taken into custody by the Princess Anne County sheriff due to "great cause of suspicion."

In July of 1706, the Princess Anne County justices ruled that Grace Sherwood would be given a trial by ducking in the Lynnhaven River. The belief at the time was that water was pure and would reject a person accused of witchcraft. If Grace was a witch she would float to the surface of the water, if she was innocent she would drown. On July 10, 1706, Grace was taken to the Lynnhaven Parish Church and was placed on a stool and ordered to ask the congregation for forgiveness for her evil ways. Grace refused. "I be not a witch, I be a healer," Grace declared.

Grace Sherwood was then marched down a dirt road now known as Witchduck Road to the mouth of the Lynnhaven River. Word of the ducking spread rapidly, and a crowd gathered to watch the spectacle. On the shoreline, Grace suffered further indignity by being stripped naked and searched by five women for any devices she may have secreted on her person to free herself from her bindings. Convinced that Grace could not free herself, the judges covered her in a sack and placed her in a boat. Grace was then rowed out 200 yards from shoreline. The justices had bound

171

Grace's right thumb to her left big toe and her left thumb to her right big toe. Before she was pushed into the river, Grace is said to have declared, "Before this day be through you will all get a worse ducking than I."

Grace was then pushed into the water. Almost immediately, Grace floated to the surface. Not satisfied by the results of the ducking, the sheriff tied a 13-pound Bible around Grace's neck. The weight of the Bible caused Grace to sink to the bottom of the river, but Grace was able to come lose from her bindings and she returned to the surface. As Grace was being pulled from the Lynnhaven River a sudden summer rain drenched the onlookers.

Following her ducking, Grace Sherwood served an unknown period in the jail next to the Lynnhaven Parish Church. Records have been lost, but it is believed that Grace was imprisoned for seven years and nine months. Grace appears to have been released by 1714. Following her release, Grace was able to get her land back from Princess Anne County with the assistance of Governor Alexander Spotswood. Grace lived quietly on her farm for the remainder of her life, dying in August or September 1740 at the age of eighty.

Today, little physical traces of the world Grace Sherwood knew can be seen in modern Virginia Beach, but her legacy is still felt. In 2006, after years of tirelessly championing Grace's story, historian Belinda Nash was successful in obtaining a pardon for Grace. On July 10, 2006, Virginia Governor Tim Kane officially pardoned Grace on the 300th anniversary of her ducking. The next year, in 2007 a statue of Grace Sherwood was dedicated on the site of Sentara Bayside Hospital. The statue shows Grace holding a basket of rosemary for her skills as a healer and with a raccoon to symbolize her love of animals. Across the street from the statue is the site of Lynnhaven Parish Church were Grace worshipped. In 2014, a memorial marker for Grace was placed in herb the garden of her former church. Every year a re-enactment of Grace Sherwood's ducking is held across from the historic Ferry Plantation House Museum. Though cleared of all charges, Grace Sherwood's restless spirit is still felt near the site of her ducking. Residents have reported seeing strange lights around the site of Grace Sherwood's ducking every July.

Grace Sherwood was a fascinating woman who stood out for her unconventional behavior. She was a skilled healer at a time when most medical treatment consisted of bleeding and purging. Her beauty and outspoken ways created jealousy and animosity in her community. She refused to be bullied and was able to survive a virtual death sentence.

Next time you are in Virginia Beach, pause for a moment and pay your respects at the statue of Grace Sherwood. Linger for a moment at Witchduck Bay. If you're lucky you might catch a glimpse of the Witch of Pungo.

Michelle L. Hamilton earned her master's degree in history from San Diego State University in 2013. In her free time, Michelle is a Civil War and 18th-century living historian. Born and raised in California, Michelle now resides in Ruther Glen, Virginia. Michelle is the author of *"I Would Still Be Drowned in Tears": Spiritualism in Abraham Lincoln's White House*, you can follow her at her blog http://michelle-hamilton.blogspot.com.

Not A Psychic
In The Parlor

Mike Ricksecker

I don't claim to be psychic. I mentioned it in an earlier chapter in the volume – I have what one may call "sensitivities" to the paranormal, but I would never claim to be a psychic medium. Friends of mine tell me that I have a lot more going on than I give myself credit, and my first ever visit to the Ferry Plantation in September 2016, is a testament to that.

First of all, I have to say that I immediately fell in love with the Ferry Plantation when I first graced its threshold. Extremely historic in a very old part of the country, it has all the charm you could ever imagine of a Nineteenth Century, Federal-style home, even though it rests smack-dab in the middle of a modern, high-class neighborhood that has tragically tried to squeeze it right out of the history books (see the Foreword for more information). Add in the mystique of the 1735 courthouse it was appended to and the 1850 extension that contains what may be the most haunted room in the whole mansion, and you have a building I could get lost in forever.

Following a paranormal convention that had been held that day, I spent the early parts of the evening getting acquainted with the house before it was opened wide for other paranormal investigators. I believe I met Bessie playing in the closet of the nursery, and Henry seemed to be home in his quarters at the very top of the old courthouse section of the mansion. I've also met Eric, the little boy who fell out of the second-floor window in what now serves as a conference room, but that was on a subsequent trip to the house the following year.

Bessie, who died at the age of seven and haunts the nursery.

It was in the best parlor that I met another resident spirit, yet it was one who had a distinct message for me.

The parlor is part of the 1850 extension of the house, and is where the family would entertain guests. It is also where they would hold wakes if someone in the family had passed away, and the caretakers of the Ferry Plantation honored that type of event by setting up a mock wake in the room. Displayed out on a long table was a faux body, and it was surrounded in the room by a handful of mourning gowns on mannequins. It was an unusual sight that one doesn't usually see set up in a historic home, but the Ferry Plantation does embrace its paranormal nature.

The mock wake set up in the best parlor.

I investigated this room on my own that evening. Other paranormal investigators were scattered about the house, and at different times I investigated with a few of them, but I wanted this room on my own. Call it a "feeling" I had.

My modest setup for this room was simply an infrared camera that I placed on the mantle, a K2 electromagnetic field detector that I placed next to the "body" on the table, a bell hanging from a chair near the piano forte (once used by Thomas Jefferson), and the digital audio recorder that I always keep strapped to my arm. That was it. I, generally, try to keep my investigations simple anyway. Less is more, in my opinion, with our bodies being the best paranormal tool we have at our disposal. That certainly became the case that night!

I started off with the usual pleasantries; I introduced myself and stated my intentions were to learn more about the house and meet the people that lived there. I have a deep respect for those souls that have passed into the afterlife, and I express that respect when I walk into their homes. It's what I would do if they were still amongst the living. I also try to learn as much about the location as I can before venturing in to investigate so that I have a much better chance of building a rapport with the spirits rather than just randomly throwing questions to the wind (I relate that method to being more like a salesman, although I understand why psychic mediums don't want to know any information beforehand). I also believe the history of a location can act as its own trigger object when you include it in our questioning.

One of the mourning gowns in the corner of the parlor, piano forte on the right.

My first topic of choice was the magnolia tree in the backyard. It was planted on April 6, 1863, by Sally Rebecca Walke as a memorial to her fiancé, John, who had fallen during the American Civil War fighting for the Confederacy. I didn't get any immediate responses to this line of conversation.

I switched my questioning to the display in front of me: the fake body. Once I asked, "What do you think of this display out here?" I got an immediate tingle, a staticky type feeling up my arms, and the room started getting very cold.

"Ok, somebody's here," I told the camera.

Spotting the white band of light.

I had the feeling that whomever had just herself known didn't like the mock wake. When I addressed this suspicion of mine, a chill ripped up my body. In the video footage, you can see me arch my back and shake it off. The presence was strong.

I could not shake the chill as I continued my questioning, the temperature seemingly dropping while I remained in the parlor talking about the display on the table before me. I had the overwhelming feeling that whomever was interacting with me was a woman and this woman did not like the display in the parlor at all. I was beginning to feel a little punch drunk, the amount of energy encompassing me casting me off into a sea of bewilderment. *What was going on? This doesn't ever happen to me.*

The woman wanted me to let the caretakers of the Ferry Plantation know that the display needed to be removed, that while, yes, wakes did occur in the parlor, they weren't the focal point of the room, and so many other good times had been had there.

I pulled my unbuttoned overshirt closed as the chill continued its icy torrent over my body. "Is there something you'd like to see here instead? You can just tell me. I have something here that might be able to pick up your voice. It's on my arm, a weird box thing that's on my arm."

At that moment, I saw some sort of white band of light float in mid-air above the window behind the body, and my audio recorder – the very device I had just been explaining could possibly pick up a voice – picked up a woman's voice that distinctly said, "Help me."

Unfortunately, I could not hear her voice at the time with my own ears, but I'd already been being made aware of the woman's desires for several minutes. The tingling sensation on my arms returned and the temperature dropped down even further.

I kept up my questioning for a while longer, but I did not see the white band of light again. I did, however, continue to feel cold and punch drunk, and the overwhelming feeling that the mock wake was disliked by the woman stayed with me.

I finally exited the best parlor, said not a word, and exited the house to catch a breather out on the park bench in the garden at the front of the mansion. Heather Moore, the director of the Ferry Plantation, found me out there a minute later and asked me what happened. I recited my tale and she proceeded to tell me that when I walked out of the parlor the other investigators there that evening saw balls of light streaming off of me.

After talking to Heather, I called my good friend, psychic medium Vanessa Hogle, to get some perspective from someone that has been experiencing this type of phenomena since the age of two. She concurred that what I experienced is one of the ways in which spirits communicate with her. She also reinforced, "See, we've been telling you that you have more going on than you give yourself credit for."

Video footage of this encounter: https://youtu.be/53X-v0t1y4s

First floor library.

Best parlor without the mock wake (2018).

First floor dining room.

Looking into the third floor nursery.

A Night At The Ferry Plantation

Rhonda Steele

The Ferry Plantation House is set in the center of the Church Point subdivision in Virginia Beach, Virginia. The houses surrounding it are half-million dollar homes, and it looks a little misplaced. The house sits on one acre that is owned by the city and is surrounded by two acres of land owned by the homeowners' association. Behind the house is an herbal garden with benches and an outside fireplace as well as a large magnolia that was planted April 6, 1863, by Sally Rebecca Walke in memory of her fiancé who was a fallen Confederate officer in the Civil War.

The site has been dated at least as far back as the Native Americans in the Sixteenth Century, including a burial ground that once rested behind the Ferry Plantation grounds.

In 1642, Savill Gaskin started the second ferry service in Hampton Roads to carry passengers on the Lynnhaven River. There is still a cannon in the river near the house that was used to signal the ferry, which had eleven stops along the river.

In this spot, the first brick courthouse was built, overall, the third courthouse in Princess Anne County. This courthouse was used until the Walke's built their home.

The Walkes had built their mansion in the 1700s but it was destroyed by a fire in 1828. It is believed that Walke ran a tavern from his home during the Revolutionary War.

The present house was built in 1830 by slave labor. It was done in Federal style with bricks used from the ruins of the original Walke manor home. Bay additions were added in 1850, one of brick and one of wood. It was covered with oyster shell stucco at one time.

The house has been used as a plantation home, courthouse, school, tavern, and a post office. It is currently a museum and an educational center.

It is reported that 11 ghosts haunt this building. These include people who died in an 1810 ship wreck at the ferry landing, Rebecca Walke, the Lady in White who supposedly died in 1826 after falling down the steps, Stella Barnett who died after eating poison mushrooms, a male slave who lived in quarters above the kitchen and still comes down to start the fire, and a cat.

It is also believed that Grace Sherwood still walks the grounds. She was called the Witch of Pungo, and was tried by ducking near this location. She was the last person tried for witchcraft in Virginia.

Mary is a little girl who has been seen frequently. Legend states that spots appear on the walls that she passes through. Eric is a little boy who fell out of a window in the late 1800s. A male servant named Henry is seen in the yard. His job was to escort house guests from the ferry landing. A nanny has been seen on the third floor, wearing a dark dress. Is she mourning one of the children? Supposedly, several children, named Margaret were born here but died shortly after birth.

Supernatural Investigators of Virginia had the opportunity to spend the night in this haunted museum. We were given a tour when we first arrived. Going up the stairs, we were hit by a strong, overpowering fish smell. Our guide said she had never smelled that before. Oysters were a commodity at the house at one time, and a sign proclaimed oysters were shucked in a room at the top of the stairs. Phantom smells, perhaps?

We were shown the room in which both Eric fell out of the window and Stella died. We were taken to the kitchen where the male slave is frequently seen, and we were also told a story about a previous investigation where a candy bar was placed on the fireplace mantel and it moved on its own. So, since we never traveled without chocolate, we placed a candy bar on the mantel and a video camera facing it. Our candy bar didn't move.

Our team took pictures, ran video cameras, and did EVP work. The kitchen is where my teammate, Tracey, had heard a cat meowing on an earlier day trip that she had taken. We captured an EVP that might sound like a cat, but it sounds more like a child calling for her mother. In the gift shop, we picked up a name: Jasper Moore. We haven't found a connection to the house with this name. Perhaps he was one of the passengers who died when the ferry shipwrecked?

Our staged candy bar did not move, but in the middle of the night some of the team were laying down on the dining room floor. They heard the rustling of candy paper but no one was eating candy. Someone had left a candy bar on the dining room table and it seems there is a Ferry Plantation spirit that likes chocolate. We recorded the sound on a digital recorder, but unfortunately, we didn't have a camera set up in that particular spot.

The parlor was used to lay out the dead for viewing. I was not able to walk into this room without my ears hurting. It felt as if I had a double ear infection and it only happened in this room.

Four of us were sitting in a room downstairs between the parlor and the dining room. The hallway to the front door and staircase was between this room and the dining room. Two of our investigators heard voices coming from the hallway. The voices were male, and it had the sound as if it was coming out of an old-fashioned radio. We verified it wasn't the investigators sleeping in the dining room and couldn't find anyone or anything that would have been talking.

We enjoyed our night at the Ferry Plantation, and we were happy to be able to take evidence with us.

The magnolia tree which was planted on April 6, 1863, by Sally Rebecca Walke as a memorial to her fiancé, John, who had fallen during the American Civil War fighting for the Confederacy.

Ferry Plantation

Vignettes

(Multiple Contributors)

<u>Cody Green</u>:

We had a team at the house one night, and Heather Moore and I were there as monitors for the house. The team found out we had a speaker set up to run an SB7 spirit box through, but it cuts out the white noise an SB7 usually generates. They asked us to set it up in the parlor and the results were immediate. Through the speaker, it actually sounded as if a party was going on in the room.

One of their investigators asked, "Should we fear death?"

A voice responded, saying, "He thinks we're dead."

I needed to step out after that, and -when I came back inside about ten minutes later the voice through the speaker said, "Is Cody still here?"

I said, "Did that just say my name?"

One of the investigators said, "That's the third time since you left."

One of the funny things about giving tours at the Ferry Plantation is many of our day time tour guests do not know it is haunted. Many times, while giving tours I have seen, heard, or felt our spirits. I will say, a few of the spirits can be goofballs, especially Stella and Cora, who are known to brush guests, who often try to play it off. The ghost cat, Whiskers, knows that I do not like cats. I give tours in a kilt, so she will walk past and wrap her tail around my leg, causing me to kick out, confusing my guests, who I am sure sometimes think I have some sort of condition. Bessie, our resident five-year old, likes to hold my hand during tours and will sometimes will swing my arm back and forth, again, causing guests to give me odd looks.

Shannon Heath:

During my first night spent at the Ferry plantation, some of us were bunking up in the nursery and it was just after everyone had fallen asleep. It was harder for me to fall asleep as fast because I was nervous and a little scared. All of a sudden, I felt something or someone crawling up between my friend's sleeping bag and mine. Then I felt a hand start to comb my hair. As freaky as it sounds, it really wasn't scary at all. This went on for a good five minutes when I realized it was one of the ghosts just trying to calm me down enough to fall asleep.

At that point, I whispered, "I know you are trying to help, but this is making me more nervous. Can you stop please?"

It stopped.

Julia Elliott

I was able to stay the night with a couple people during a paranormal investigation at the Ferry Plantation. We were getting ready for bed, and I was standing in the library looking into the dining room. I saw a woman dressed in a big-bottomed grey and white dress with a bonnet on her head walk from one end of the room to the other and walk right into the wall. I've seen a lot of spirits, but nothing like this. This looked like a real person; she even had color to her face. It was insane.

We ended up sleeping on air mattresses in the library. Everyone had gone to sleep, but I couldn't fall asleep because I felt like someone was standing over me. It wasn't a bad feeling, it was just very prominent.

I finally fell asleep between 3:00 – 4:00 AM and was woken up to something standing on my air mattress. It felt like a full-grown adult had stepped on it because the entire thing shifted.

Once I woke up, I heard what sounded like Indian flute music and drums coming from outside. Maybe I was exhausted, but I could've sworn I saw fire light coming from way in the backyard.

I went back to sleep after that. I had a dream I was standing in front of myself and friend, sleeping, and there was a woman's voice telling me, "Everything you see and feel about these spirits are true."

In the dream I had an African American man and an older woman standing beside me. I believe the man was Henry [who lived in the space above the Loom Room], but I'm not sure about the woman. It was the most intense paranormal experience I have ever had.

Ferry Plantation
Roundtable

Amanda Donaldson, Cody Green, and
Brennan Guenzel

Mike Ricksecker:

Members of ACID Paranormal have been helping take care of the Ferry Plantation for a number of years and have had quite a few paranormal experiences. Following the ParaCon at the Ferry event in September 2018, I sat down with Amanda Donaldson, Cody Green, and Brennan Guenzel to talk about the encounters they've had during their time there.

Note: There are frequent references in the conversation to Heather Moore, who was unavailable for this interview but sits on the board and has been instrumental in the operations of the Ferry Plantation, and Belinda Nash, historian, authors, and long-time director of the plantation who passed away in 2016 but is the one who worked tirelessly in making the Ferry Plantation the amazing living history museum it is today and was instrumental in the pardoning of Grace Sherwood in 2006.

Of the three different sections of the house (1735, 1830, 1850), which do you find the most active?

Cody Green:
The 1850 and the parlor.

Brennan Guenzel:
The parlor is probably the most active. That's where if we set up spirit boxes, any kind of equipment, it's always in there you get most of the activity.

That's where's I've gotten a lot of my activity and most of my experiences, so why do you think the parlor?

Amanda Donaldson:
I think it was just the most visited room; it's where they spent most of their time. We have the 11 resident spirits, but that's not all we get sometimes. Sometimes we've been able to channel the spirits of Thomas Jefferson and Lafayette who have been visitors on the property, so I think it's because that's where they would have spent most of their time while they were here.

Cody Green:
I think the piano forte helps with that, too. The energy around that thing – it was in a tavern that Thomas Jefferson frequented, and then it ended up in a barn in Smithfield, and then Belinda chased it down and purchased it. So, it's been around since... well, Thomas Jefferson. Thomas Jefferson came to the property because he was Rebecca Walke's first cousin. He would come out here for the quiet and to get away from the politics.

Amanda Donaldson:
It's rumored that part of the Declaration of Independence was written here.

Cody Green:
Because it was a secret place for him to go, it would make sense – at least notes, it's a place of reflection. The manor house was still here, so he had a place to stay when he was down here. That place

was massive. He could find a quiet place in there and get away from everything, an no one knew he was here.

The piano forte used by Thomas Jefferson.

And the manor house burned down in…?

Cody Green:
1828. There was a party, and they got a little too drunk and knocked over an oil lamp. Then the fire hit the whale oil in the basement and boom.

So… 11 resident spirts. Who are the 11 resident spirits?

Cody Green:
There's Isabella, Bessie, Eric, Henry, Chloe…

Amanda Donaldson:
Stella, Cora, Charles McIntosh, Charles Barnett, the nanny…

Brennan Guenzel:
Charles Walke.

Cody Green:
Those are the resident ones. There are others that will come and go. One that comes and goes came by today: Belinda.

Belinda comes by?

Cody Green:
Oh, yeah. We'll catch her perfume. The first time, I was catching a floral perfume and Heather comes in and says, "Belinda's here."

Grace Sherwood isn't one of the 11 resident spirits?

Cody Green:
She comes by, but she's not a resident spirit. The real connections to the property were the use of our ferry right here on the Lynnhaven [River], and then Belinda who saved this house from demolition and got Grace pardoned.

Brennan Guenzel:
She was also a parishioner of Old Donation Church which was on the property at the time.

Cody Green:
It was called that because the Walke's donated the land to the church. And the court house she was tried at was right next to the church.

Amanda Donaldson:
So, the property as we think of it today… we have a very small piece of the property. Is she attached to what is here today? No. She is connected to, in a sense, a portion of the original property that was owned at that time by the family.

Cody Green:
This property was 15,000 acres, which is huge.

Where's the jail for *this* courthouse? [Note: The 1735 section of the Ferry Plantation was originally a small courthouse, added on to for use as a home after the original manor house burned down.]

Cody Green:
Underneath the courthouse. The shackles and keys and bayonet in the window are from the excavation. The closet [in the kitchen] under the stairs once had stairs that led down to the jail, but it was all floored over when the last family, Mrs. Halloran, lived here.

Brendan Guenzel:
Also, when they were doing the restoration of the house, they found this [bayonet in sheath] in the wall by where the old fireplace was.

Cody Green:
When Mrs. Halloran lived here the fireplace was actually walled off. They didn't know a fireplace was there; her range sat in front of it. That attributes to the story of what her doctor told people.

The kitchen fireplace which was uncovered and restored.

She had a live-in caretaker, so twice each year her doctor would give the caretaker two weeks off, and the doctor would come to live with Mrs. Halloran. In the winter, he sat in the nook in the kitchen having his evening coffee, and a large, black man who we now know as Henry would come out of the wall where the staircase [leading to the second floor "loom room"] is, walk over to the range was as if it wasn't there, lean over like we was stoking a fire, stand up, nod to the doctor, and then would go back into the wall.

It would always happen in the winter, which would make sense as that chimney goes all the way up to Henry's room [third floor], and he would want to keep that fire going to keep his room warm.

What are your most significant experiences at the Ferry Plantation?

Amanda Donaldson:
My favorite is the first time I was touched ever by anything paranormal. We had a Girl Scout troop that spent the night. Now, when the Girl Scouts come we don't focus on the paranormal; it's more about the history, they get to make cool crafts, and there's actually a Ferry Plantation Girl Scout badge they can earn.

Heather was going to be there that night, and she asked if we could make it a girl's night, so this was actually the first time I got to spend the night in the house. Since it was my first time, she asked where I would like to stay, and I wanted to stay in the nursery. Come time to go to bed, there were three of us that went upstairs with our sleeping bags, Heather, another volunteer at the time, Shannon, and I. We laid our sleeping bags out, and I'd say there was a good foot to a foot and a half between us. I'm laying there, and all of a sudden, I feel a tug-tug-tug on my sleeping bag. I looked over to see if Heather was messing with me, but nobody was, so I rolled back over, and it happened again – tug-tug-tug.

It was Bessie. I literally had to lift my sleeping bag up, I felt her crawl into the sleeping bag with me and wrap her arm around my waist.

Cody Green:
She [Bessie] seems to be the most active. She likes to mess with me when I'm giving regular history tours. She'll grab two of my fingers and swing like a kid does, and people will look at me like I'm crazy.

Brennan Guenzel:
The biggest one for me was up in Henry's room. Heather and I, along with an investigator named Sebastian, and we were just sitting there chatting. For some reason, Sebastian got on the topic of religion and saying how he knows people believe in it but he doesn't believe in heaven in hell when, suddenly, a K2 meter that we had set up in the middle of the room on a box went flying off the box and hit the brick wall on the other side of the room. Of course, after that happened, we gave him a hard time and asked him if he believes in Jesus now!

Cody Green:
For me, the craziest one was with Heather and I, we were waiting for a paranormal team to show up but they were running a little late, so I walked out to the parking lot to smoke a cigarette. There was fog, but there was no wind, it just sitting there, this thick fog. By the time I finished walking out to the parking lot, I saw a ship sitting out in the water, which can't happen anymore. I sent Heather a text and told her, "You need to come out here right now."

She came out there right next to me, and I pointed to it and said, "What do you see?"

"Is that a ship?"

It was an old, wooden tall ship. We were just standing there looking at it, and I felt all kinds of energy passing me, like people were just walking past me. Heather turned to walk back to the house, and I called after her, "Heather!"

She turned back around and the ship and the fog were gone. I had turned slightly when she started walking back, and in the moment, like I had blinked, it was all gone. And there was no wind.

So, we started walking up to the house and there were wet footprints leading up to the house. In front of the river side door there was a puddle like people had been shaking off before going inside.

The Ferry Plantation from the air, nestled amongst the modern homes, with Virginia Beach and a storm looming in the background.

Conclusion

Mike Ricksecker

There never really is a conclusion, although we must set aside a moment to wrap up this particular volume and give pause until the next, but the supernatural realm never rests. It is always around us, always a part of us, and at times, we capture a small glimpse of it when we have an encounter, as described amongst the myriad of stories contained within this text.

While many believe the final frontier is space – and that may be true in a physical sense – I believe the final frontier is a non-physical one, a frontier in other dimensions and a spiritual plane of existence (all religions aside) that we're still learning to access and explore. Admitting the truth to ourselves that these paranormal experiences are real is the first step in gaining access to that world. I also believe that our historic locations, with all the energy of lives gone by stored within, can serve as gateways to access that world we are blind to in our everyday lives.

We may be four volumes into this Encounters With The Paranormal journey, but we've just started traveling down the haunted road.

Other titles from Haunted Road Media:

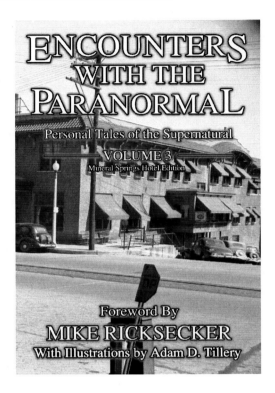

Almost everyone has a ghost story. Real people. Real stories.

In this third volume, read about more haunted houses, supernatural creatures, messages from pets from the other side, haunted history, experiences during paranormal investigations, psychic experiences, and more, including a dedicated section to the historic Mineral Springs Hotel. ENCOUNTERS WITH THE PARANORMAL: VOLUME 3 reveals more personal stories of the supernatural and paranormal, continuing to explore the realm beyond the veil through its contributors.

Explore With Us and Discover Real Paranormal Experiences!

The Haunted Road Media YouTube channel has over 500 paranormal videos, two live stream shows, full paranormal investigation videos, ghost stories, and more!

Subscribe at: http://www.youtube.com/hauntedroadmedia

For more information visit:
www.hauntedroadmedia.com

Made in United States
North Haven, CT
11 November 2021

11045296R00114